GARDEN FAVORITES

GARDEN FAVORITES

Designing with Herbs, Climbers, Roses, and Grasses

Warren Schultz

Rebecca W. Atwater Briccetti

Rick Darke

MetroBooks

MetroBooks

An Imprint of the Michael Friedman Publishing Group, Inc.

Library of Congress Cataloging-in-Publication Data available upon request.

ISBN 1-56799-778-3

Introduction: Penelope O'Sullivan
Editors: Reka Simonsen, Susan Lauzau, Stephen Slaybaugh, Kelly Matthews
Art Directors: Jeff Batzli and Lynne Yeamans
Designers: Charles Donahue, Meredith Miller, Robbi Oppermann Firestone, Maria Mann, Stan Stanski
Photography Director: Christopher C. Bain
Photography Editors: Wendy Missan, Colleen Branigan, Valerie E. Kennedy
Production Managers: Ingrid Neimanis-McNamara and Camille Lee

Color separations by Fine Arts Repro House Co., Ltd.
Printed in China by Leefung-Asco Printers Ltd.

3 5 7 9 10 8 6 4 2

For bulk purchases and special sales, please contact:
Michael Friedman Publishing Group, Inc.
Attention: Sales Department
230 Fifth Avenue
New York, NY 10001
212/685-6610   FAX 212/685-3916

Visit our website:
www.metrobooks.com

Table of Contents

INTRODUCTION

Timeless gardens linger in the memory long after one has strolled through them or explored their secrets in a book. They capture our imaginations, creating in us the desire to visit them again and again. We want to see how they change from season to season, we long to understand what makes them work.

Inevitably, it's the plants that make these gardens special, bringing their particular magic to each garden situation. In Garden Favorites, you'll discover the romance of herbs, vines and climbers, roses, and ornamental grasses. Each of these plant types brings distinctive color, form, and beauty to the garden.

Design is also an important factor in the creation of an enduring garden, as it determines how to use each plant for its finest effect. Good garden design takes into account the nature of each plant—its height, color, and form, as well as its cultural requirements for light and soil—to create an all-encompassing plan where healthy plants can grow and flourish.

One garden that has withstood the test of time is the herb garden. Since ancient times, gardeners have grown herbs not just for their beauty but for their practicality. Herbs like echinacea and valerian form the basis of popular medicines. The proverbial parsley, sage, rosemary, and thyme, along with many other tasty herbs, make delicious additions to various national cuisines. In medieval times, lavender and similarly fragrant herbs were sometimes strewn to mask unpleasant odors in earthy peasant huts and lordly homes alike. Lavender is still popular today, found in many potpourris, soaps, and furniture polishes.

Traditional herb gardens tend to be geometrical in shape, with the plants arranged for easy care and collection. Often, a simple parterre design is well suited for herbs, since many are evergreen or semi-evergreen, and hold some color and form through the winter. Herb gardens, however,

OPPOSITE: Herbs make a nice addition to any garden—they don't have to be consigned to a small plot near the kitchen. In this lush garden, a variety of cooking herbs fills in the spaces between bright flowers.

ABOVE: A single vibrant bloom from an orange clock vine heralds summer in all its glory. With such rich color and dramatic shape, just one of these hardy climbers can make a simple garden extraordinary.

can be as modern as the gardener who grows them, bringing color to meadow plantings and lushness to beds and borders. Because herb gardens predate medieval monasteries and travel back in time beyond ancient Greece and Rome, they offer a romantic sense of connection with the past and convey their beauty and lore to future generations.

While herb gardening instills an appreciation for the function and history of herbs, gardening with vines and climbers has a very different effect. With their clinging vertical nature, vines project a lust for growth and movement. The vigor of vines that twine and scramble over trees,

shrubs, porches, and trellises recalls life's unstoppable progress through seasons of growth and change. On a practical level, vines and climbers are a fast and easy way to provide quick shade and to fill vertical space. Foliage vines like ivy can soften the lines of a building year-round. Vines and climbers can also have a short-term or seasonal effect. The flowers of clematis and climbing roses, for example, create an attractive display during the summer, with the bloom time dependent on the variety.

Roses need not be attached to arbors or trellises to add immeasurable beauty to the landscape. These garden classics carry with them an ancient

OPPOSITE: No other plant captures our hearts and imaginations the way the rose does. Ramblers such as this lovely pink 'Etain' bring fragrance and beauty to even the plainest garden fence.

ABOVE: Grasses come in an astonishing range of colors. In this autumnal garden, the warm golden tones of the fountain grass, *Pennisetum alopecuroides,* create a bright backdrop for the coppery hues of the switch grass, *Panicum virgatum.*

tradition of landscape use and add a sense of timelessness to the flower garden. Their perfection of form, color, and fragrance makes roses indispensable in formal beds and casual mixed borders. Their habit ranges from spreading ground covers and massive shrubs to miniature bushes no bigger than a flowering impatiens. Blossoms vary from blowzy, carefree, once-blooming old garden roses with hundreds of petals to refined hybrid teas with long-stemmed, high-centered, repeating blooms. Roses go well with other roses, but they can also be breathtaking when planted with companions like foxglove, lilies, rue, lavender, boxwood, berberis, or certain ornamental grasses.

Indeed, ornamental grasses are extraordinary in their own right. The sight of massed grasses rippling in a gentle breeze is memorable in summer, autumn, and winter. Backlit by the rising or setting sun, their inflorescences of pink, silver, or beige shimmer on delicate stems. In winter especially, tall grasses like Miscanthus look dramatic with their faded leaves and flowers coated in glistening ice and tipped with snow. Grasses provide year-round textures from fine to coarse and, during the growing season, their colors can range from variegated green and white to blood red and glaucous blue. Forms vary from tight and spiky to loose, fountain-like, or spreading. Small clumping grasses are excellent for edging and grouping, while big varieties—sometimes ten feet tall or more—make for statuesque garden accents and stunning masses. The enduring appeal of grasses, however, must derive from their close relationship with nature. Intimately connected with the earth, they belong in any landscape, quivering in the slightest breeze, bending with snow and ice, and turning tawny when the earth browns in fall.

Each chapter of this book illustrates a unique dimension of ageless garden beauty. Let these photographs of grasses, herbs, roses, and vines inspire you to dream, to design, and to act. Enjoy their enduring splendor and classic designs. Whether you garden on an estate or in a window box, you will discover fresh ideas that you can adapt or incorporate into a favorite garden of your own.

OPPOSITE: Japanese wisteria adds heady fragrance and a sense of romance to any house or garden, whether climbing up the façade of a brick mansion or growing as a tree in a front yard. White wisteria is lovely in a garden with many other flowers, but the lavender-hued variety is best for those places where a single, dramatic spot of color is called for.

Part One
HERB GARDENS

INTRODUCTION

*H*erb gardens are among the oldest of recorded gardens. For thousands of years gardens were created to cultivate useful plants; the conceit of the purely ornamental garden is thought to be merely centuries old. It is their usefulness that characterizes herbs in the first place. What is an herb? It is a plant valued for some power. It may have admirable flowers or handsome foliage, but it is prized for more than that. We look to herbs for comfort and refreshment. We use them for remedies and as purifying agents. They provide dyes and inks and decoration of all kinds. Their fragrances may stimulate or soothe. And their culinary contributions are beyond reckoning.

Many plants once considered herbs are thought of as ornamentals today. Consider the rose, which has a long and venerable history in the preparation of food, remedies, and cosmetics. Petals of the apothecary's rose (Rosa gallica officinalis) have been used in astringents and antiseptics, and to treat pulmonary disease and sore throats. Other roses lend their fragrance to perfumes and potpourris. Rose water, rarely used today in Western cooking, was once indispensable. In the twentieth century, few people are accustomed to thinking of the rose as an herb, and so it is with many, many other plants. Yet the number of plants that may be considered herbs is tremendous.

Not everyone will look on the plants featured in these pages the same way. For some, their traditional characteristics as herbs will be fascinating. Others will appreciate their ornamental contributions to the flower border and tabletop arrangements. Plant them exclusively for the classic, most narrowly defined herb garden or let them provide the framework for an ornamental kitchen garden. Place them in the landscape in wildly diverse plantings. For the most part, herbs are forgiving and of fairly easy culture. Many are drought-tolerant, quite hardy, or both. If a vigorous groundcover is desired, herbs offer numerous possibilities. What group of plants is so versatile and accommodating?

ABOVE: A regal, or royal, lily (*Lilium regale*), nicotiana, and assorted herbs by the kitchen window offer fragrance to the slightest breeze. Keep culinary herbs close at hand so it isn't a chore to fetch them when in the midst of cooking.

OPPOSITE: A massive planting of purple sage at their feet makes the bright spires of desert candle (*Eremurus himalaicus*) all the more dramatic. Raised beds, in this case edged by railroad ties, have the advantage of improved drainage, and they also serve to direct attention to the plants they contain.

ABOVE: In a majestic combination, 'Hidcote' lavender and a rich red variety of pink campion (*Lychnis coronaria*) look splendid massed in the landscape.

OPPOSITE: A scattering of golden-leaved feverfew (*Tanacetum parthenium* 'Aureum') gleams in this spring tapestry. Tulips punctuate the end of a tiny path that leads to a sundial.

ABOVE: The daisylike flowers of feverfew (*Tanacetum parthenium*) are offset by herbaceous *Potentilla* and *Achillea*. Native to southeastern Europe, feverfew was brought to North America as an ornamental, and is a favorite combined with dark green foliage plants.

OPPOSITE: This evergreen bay tree (*Laurus nobilis*) in a square pot is surrounded by the soft pastels of *Pelargonium* 'Apple Blossom Orbit' and *Viola* 'Paper White'. The potted standard and radial design give this tiny garden a formal air.

TRADITIONAL HERB GARDENS

The earliest herb gardens were enclosed and often of circular, square, or rectangular design. The classic atrium and peristyle of the ancient world eventually gave way to the courtyard and cloister, often a square with a cross at its center defined by paths. In gardens of the Middle Ages, the beds were laid out in straight lines and at right angles. Plants were grown for study, or for physical or spiritual treatment; the garden of one secluded religious order dating to the eighth century included savory, lily, poppy, iris, burdock, clary, houseleek (Sempervivum tectorum), and marsh mallow.

The Renaissance garden saw increasingly elaborate curving lines within the rectilinear framework, and symmetry—which had played an understated role in the medieval garden—became a theme of rich ornamentation. Intricate designs were created and "filled in" with contrasting plants. The axes of the Renaissance garden were usually consistent with the axes of the building around which they were designed, and the garden was intended to be viewed from a raised terrace or from within the building. Garden design of this period often featured the symmetrical pattern of planted beds known as parterres, in which the design described by living plants was grown in relief in a field of crushed stone or shells.

The knot garden, also popular about this time, featured low-growing, often shrubby plants set in interweaving geometric patterns. In mild climates, hedges of rosemary and lavender can be used to define the "knots," but boxwood, santolina, hyssop, germander, thyme, and marjoram are more commonly used.

Herb gardens of the colonial era were a far simpler affair, a reflection of the means of their owners. Though usually "working" gardens, they were often true to the love of symmetry; many were based on the popular design of a square divided into triangles by intersecting paths of brick or gravel. In the traditional herb garden today, herbs tend to dominate; or they may share the limelight with vegetables, as in the kitchen garden. Such a garden might contain a vast collection of herbs or only a few choice favorites. Yet even though the twentieth-century herb garden might be designed as nothing more complicated than a hardy border, the herb garden remains the domain of plants we single out as special.

ABOVE: Lush ribbons of chive plants fashion handsome borders for this colonial potager. The rounded flower clusters, in shades of purple, lavender, pink, or white, sit above blue-green tubular foliage that falls in soft fans. Chives offer a very effective contrast to the other members of this kitchen garden.

OPPOSITE: Geometric beds can give plants of great size or exuberant habit the room they need to thrive within the context of a rather formal garden scheme. This raised bed garden ensures well-drained soil for box, peppermint, green fennel, and spectacular bronze fennel. Raised beds are a time-honored tradition in gardening, dating at least to the middle of the fifteenth century. Gravel paths make for a well-ordered appearance and easy harvest.

ABOVE: Walkways of old brick complement garden plantings of many moods, which can be designed separately in their own compartments. In this garden, coriander, clary sage, and rosemary stand out against a formal clipped hedge.

OPPOSITE: All basil varieties thrive in sunny, well-drained locations—an excellent spot for the kitchen garden. This practical grouping, which contrasts the expected emerald green of several common basils with the dramatic purple-red of *Osimum basilicum* 'Purpurasens', makes it possible to harvest a delicious assortment for kitchen use all at once.

ABOVE: Herb garden plants needn't be confined to beds. These cheerful nasturtiums tumble around a weathered bench for a playful, rustic effect.

RIGHT: Here, a traditional circular herb garden design is punctuated at its center with an urn raised on a pedestal. Wide paths of brick give this garden scene, with its great variety of plants, a feeling of unity. The dramatic height of the urn isn't out of place, as several of the plantings themselves are quite tall, and the whole picture is backed by a stately hedge.

ABOVE: Here, an old wagon wheel provides the inspiration for a showcase of thymes, among them coconut thyme, woolly thyme, alba thyme, and clear gold thyme. It is easy to mistake a number of thyme varieties, and the spokes of this wheel keep the little "beds" quite separate, a nice idea for those who want to experiment in their cooking.

OPPOSITE: A rock wall garden can provide a growing site with excellent drainage. This ornamental planting combines the salad herbs parsley, borage, and purple basil with marigold, Johnny jump-up, and *Rosa rugosa* blossoms. Nasturtiums peek into the scene from the right. Although the plants are tucked into this rockery at various levels, all are within easy reach for harvest.

ABOVE: Perfectly straight rows give this beautifully tended vegetable garden a practical aspect, and certainly this design makes cultivation and harvesting as easy as can be. Formally clipped shrubs growing alongside the paved garden path echo the pleasing symmetry and recall the gardens of the sixteenth and seventeenth centuries, when flower and vegetable beds grew side by side in stylized parterres.

ABOVE: Culinary herbs, here a trio of thymes—golden, purple variegated, and white—are best grown in quantity if they are to be harvested regularly. A billowing profusion of growth spills over the sides of these geometrical raised beds.

ABOVE: In cottage gardens, where useful herbs and purely ornamental flowers grow chockablock, taller plants and those with more massive foliage are not always relegated to the very back row, as they are in more traditional beds.

OPPOSITE: This combination of chives (*Allium schoenoprasum*), salvia, and white-leaf everlasting, or curry plant (*Helichrysum angustifolium*), offers flowers and foliage for drying and for flavoring vinegars, salads, and other culinary offerings. It provides plenty of interesting additions to fresh flower arrangements as well.

ABOVE: A low parterre of clipped boxwood is filled with various herbs. The varying colors and textures of the herbs are reminiscent of a well-worked tapestry, proving that herbs can be used luxuriantly in even the most formal of settings.

OPPOSITE: The foliage of parsley 'Bravour' here resembles nothing so much as a miniature deciduous forest in autumn. For thousands of years, parsley has held a place of enormous importance in kitchen gardens.

ABOVE: In this enchanting English garden, such medieval herb-garden plants as fennel and foxglove (*Digitalis lutea*) grow in a more contemporary border setting. This bed's relaxed feel lends itself well to the more natural landscaping of many gardens today.

OPPOSITE: This arrangement of jewel-toned herbs rivals that of any flower border, with all the variety of texture a gardener could wish for. The happy confusion of fennel, purple sage, various alliums, and lavender (*Lavandula stoechas*) is kept quietly in check with traditional pavers set in orderly fashion.

ABOVE: This potager combines the decorative effect of a formal parterre with the virtues of a working kitchen garden. A standard gooseberry punctuates the little central disk. Individual beds supply the owners with such diverse crops as onions, sorrel, and mint, and fragrant honeysuckle abundantly covers the fence.

OPPOSITE: A popular theme is that of the Shakespeare garden, which features plants mentioned by the author in his plays and poems. Planted in these lush beds formally crisscrossed by stone paths are sweet cicely, alecost (*Chrysanthemum balsamita* or *Balsamita major*), and the ever-popular fennel. The style of this garden, with its rectilinear layout and low-growing, clipped borders, complements that of the house even though it is not a slavish period reproduction.

HERBS IN THE LANDSCAPE

*I*n recent centuries it has been the fashion to confine herbs to gardens devoted exclusively to their kind—that is, gardens of "useful" plants. But remembering that the plants we know as herbs hail from scores of families and are amazingly diverse, it should come as no surprise that many of them stand beautifully on their own and look marvelous when integrated into the rest of the garden. After all, you can choose among herbs anything from shrubs and even trees to groundcovers. They offer flowers of every description, and often foliage that is beautifully ornamental, perhaps with unusual texture or intriguing shape, glaucous or in beguiling tones of blue.

In mixed borders, larger groupings of herbs make an impressive display. In perennial gardens, many herbs can be called on to provide contrast and to fill in where immature plantings have yet to grow. Many of the shorter plants are pretty in an uncommon way for edging walkways or beds; the tallest can make striking accents in the landscape. And for the fancier of the wildflower, hummingbird, or butterfly garden, herbs are simply indispensable.

ABOVE: Herbs and ornamentals spill over the sides of this time-worn brick walkway. The low, mounding habit of many herbs makes them convenient companions around a garden seat, from which the butterflies and bees they attract can be enjoyed.

OPPOSITE: A sundial, reached by stepping stones that are nearly overgrown, stands in this romantic herbaceous border, which includes feverfew, santolina, violets, and French lavender. It is easy to forget the working nature of herbs when we see them so gracefully integrated into such a magnificent composition.

ABOVE: Thyme, planted among the paving stones in this quiet corner, acts in concert with a sundial to make the age-old pun on "time." A rustic bench offers a serene spot for contemplation.

ABOVE: Mounds of cranesbill (*Geranium psilostemon*) and golden marjoram (*Origanum vulgare* 'Aureum') are anchors in this fabulous garden planned around yellows, greens, and white. The herb isn't tucked into an inconspicuous corner, but is literally allowed to shine.

ABOVE: The accommodating climate of the Pacific Northwest coaxes a wide variety of ornamentals and herbs to perform at their best. Stately yellow iris are answered at the back of this garden by fox-gloves, and fennel and roses are unexpected companions in the foreground.

OPPOSITE: Herbs integrated into this extraordinary border are on a par with the best-known of ornamentals. Featured here are *Euphorbia characias, E. wulfenii,* purple sage, *Kniphofia* 'August Yellow', and *Artemisia* 'White Windows'. The sage makes a striking contribution.

ABOVE: These white tulips are spotlit by lemon balm. Where climate allows, tuck herbs into the spring flower border. They'll offer a longer season of usefulness with such an early start, and the variety of foliage will be most welcome.

LEFT: A ramble through an earthly paradise reveals a splashy planting of herbs. *Nepeta sibirica* weaves among plantings of two roses—*Rosa gallica officinalis* and *R. mundi*—resulting in a scene so saturated with color that it looks as though it were drawn in pastels.

ABOVE: Many herbs make excellent underplantings. Here, individual orange trees are centered in their own little beds.

OPPOSITE: A slope covered with relatively easygoing plants is a practical answer to erosion. When considering an alternative to grass, let your imagination run wild. Few herbs demand meticulous attention, and many are quite water-thrifty.

ABOVE: In this nod to the cottage garden, flowers in every shade of purple are offset by a great diversity of foliage, much of it a bright lime green. It is the dramatic heads of flowering chives (*Allium*) that get the most attention here.

RIGHT: Border "hedges" of 'Hidcote' lavender line the axes of a formal composition that features standard roses. Sorrel (*Rumex*), a tender green with a bright, acidic flavor, surrounds a potted olive tree. In a mild climate, a garden such as this can be enjoyed for many months.

ABOVE: This little planting of herbs and ornamentals is a living nosegay. The hot colors of red and orange-gold are more than matched by the enthusiastic diversity of foliage. Flower umbels of dill add an airy note to an otherwise dense collection.

OPPOSITE: Columbine (*Aquilegia*), alecost (*Chrysanthemum balsamita*), catmint (*Nepeta*), and wormwood (*Artemisia absinthum*) are combined in this beautifully designed Shakespeare garden, a collection with great variety of foliage and flower.

ABOVE: Rosemary (*Rosmarinus officinalis*) and thick-leaf phlox (*Phlox carolina* 'Chattahoochee') seem unusual partners at this entryway, perhaps because rosemary's culinary fame overshadows its distinguished past as an ornamental. It will grow quite shrubby, and lends itself nicely to topiary.

LEFT: A hedge gateway invites the visitor into this stunning garden of purples and pinks. *Nepeta* and *Dianthus* traditionally appear in perennial borders such as these. Depending on the species (of which there are hundreds), *Dianthus* can offer rich, spicy fragrance, blue-green foliage, and abundant flowering, all in one rather low-growing plant that masses beautifully. *D. caryophyllus*, known as clove pink for its fragrance, was used to scent and flavor cosmetic and medicinal preparations for centuries.

THE WORKING NATURE
OF HERBS

*P*lant a variety of herbs, and you will not exhaust the possibilities for their uses for a long while. A home supply of herbs is a delirious resource for anyone with an interest in cooking or handicrafts. There is nothing more inspiring to the cook than a garden full of flavorful herbs, which are delightful in salads, sauces, soups, and indeed almost any dish. In the depths of winter, dried herbs rekindle the fresh tastes of summer, easing us through harsh and unruly weather with promises that the garden will prosper again.

As adornments for wreaths, bouquets, and other ornamental arrangements, herbs—both fresh and dried—have their decorative uses outside the garden. They also make a fragrant and colorful contribution to many pot-pourris and perfumes.

Traditionally, herbs have also been used in soothing teas as well as medicinally in syrups and extractions. The dual nature of these time-honored plants, which are both ornamental and hardworking, makes them extraordinarily rewarding garden dwellers.

ABOVE: Anise hyssop (*Agastache foeniculum*), planted in generous clumps, makes itself noticed in the garden; when the plant—also known as blue or fennel giant hyssop—is happy, it may reach three feet (90cm) tall. A hardy member of the mint family and not a true hyssop, it is unrelated to the plant that flavored homemade cough syrups. The clean green leaves, which may be dried for use in cooking and in making tea, have a complex flavor that, like licorice or anise, seems faintly sweet. The flowers make pretty garnishes and are delicious in baked goods and sautés; they grow in substantial purple spikes that attract butterflies, bees, and hummingbirds in mid- to late summer.

OPPOSITE: Chamomile and other herbs provide a ground-covering carpet beneath the branches of this standard gooseberry. A standard of any kind is an elegant accent for a circular bed, and any number of low-growing herbs would serve double duty planted around the base, in the place of the more usual flowering annuals.

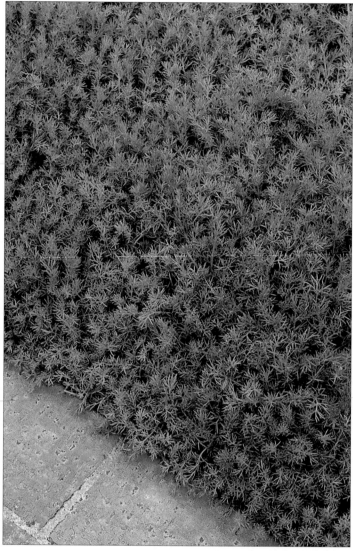

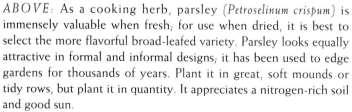

ABOVE: As a cooking herb, parsley (*Petroselinum crispum*) is immensely valuable when fresh; for use when dried, it is best to select the more flavorful broad-leafed variety. Parsley looks equally attractive in formal and informal designs; it has been used to edge gardens for thousands of years. Plant it in great, soft mounds or tidy rows, but plant it in quantity. It appreciates a nitrogen-rich soil and good sun.

ABOVE: In early to midsummer, chamomile produces tiny, daisy-like flowers, long used in soothing teas and other preparations. The soft, almost wispy foliage forms a feathery mound when plants are set close together. Roman chamomile (*Chamaemelum nobile*) and German, or sweet false, chamomile (*Matricaria recutita*) look much alike. German chamomile, a true annual, can reach two feet (60cm) in height, producing flowers less bitter than those of the one-foot (30cm) Roman chamomile, a tender perennial. Roman chamomile foliage is often described as apple-scented.

ABOVE: Lemon mint (*Mentha xpiperita*, also known as *M. citrata*) goes by the common name of bergamot mint as well. The leaves of this somewhat shorter (eighteen to twenty-four inches [45 to 60cm]) pepper-mint variety have a lemony aroma when bruised. The commercial zenith of lemon mint was eighteenth-century France, where it was used in the preparation of a vast array of cosmetics, perfumes, and potpourris. In the garden, it offers masses of lush emerald growth that can be held in check—if, for example, bordered by bricks or paving stones.

ABOVE: Harvest lavender where it grows in profusion, to avoid stripping the plants. Slender flower spikes and narrow leaves make lavender an elegant addition to cut-flower arrangements; the combination of dusty, faded purple blossoms and gray-green leaves is sophisticated, whether fresh or dried. Lavender is the herb of choice for scenting linens and soaps, and culinary tradition in some parts of the world, perhaps most famously Provence, uses it to flavor savories and sweets.

ABOVE LEFT: Chicory flowers, composed of delicate purple, daisylike rays, emerge along weedy, open stems. Their spare contribution is prettiest in combination with more fulsome plants. Members of the chicory family have been enjoyed in cooking for thousands of years—the leaves in salads, the roots eaten boiled or raw as a vegetable, or roasted and ground as a coffee substitute (of debatable success). *Cichorium* has historically been used as a medicine in treating heart and circulatory ailments.

ABOVE RIGHT: Scented geraniums (*Pelargonium*) number more than two hundred, and a tremendous variety of fragrances are commercially available. Choose from geraniums with scents reminiscent of citrus and spices of many kinds, various nuts, mints, stone fruits, ginger, and rose, among others. New hybrids appear with every passing year. The foliage can look as glorious as it smells, sometimes elaborately ruffled, variegated, or handsomely margined. Scented geraniums thrive in the garden (provide for good air circulation), and brought indoors in containers, their rich fragrance can be enjoyed close at hand.

LEFT: This corner of a kitchen garden features a pretty arrangement of chives, feverfew, and santolina. Various cultures, among them Chinese, Arab, and western European, have found medicinal uses for these herbs over the years. Today santolina, or lavender cotton, is more valued as an ornamental that lends itself to neat management; it has long been used in knot gardens. The very bitter nature of feverfew discourages any use but therapeutic, leaving chives the sole member of this grouping truly welcome at the table.

ABOVE: What garden would be complete without dill *(Anethum graveolens)*? It has a distinguished presence in the herb garden, and is a soft and starry addition to the back of the flower border. The yellow-green flower umbels are fireworks displays in miniature. The foliage and flowers taste of the very essence of summer, and the richly fragrant seeds keep handily to flavor breads, salads, soups, and pickles in the cooler months. A rewarding herb to raise from seed, dill should be sown where it is intended to grow, as it doesn't like to be transplanted.

ABOVE: The flowers of garlic chives (*Allium tuberosum*) resemble those of certain heat-loving, subtropical bulbs, but these plants are much more accepting of variable weather. Harvest young leaves (wider and flatter than those of the herb simply known as "chives") for the gentle flavor of garlic they add to foods. The blooms make a stunning addition to flower arrangements.

RIGHT: No herb is so winning when eaten fresh, nor so disappointing by contrast when dried, as basil. Sweet basil 'Green Ruffles' (*Ocimum basilicum*) is one of the huge number of cultivars commercially available. The flavors of lemon, cinnamon, and anise basils make a nice change, and basils with purple foliage are a delight. Thai basil produces delicious leaves as long as three inches (7cm), and at eighteen to twenty-four inches (45 to 60cm) tall, is a handsome foliage plant in the landscape; it is described as tasting of mint and cloves. As basil is rather slow to grow from seed, you may want to seek out young plants for your garden.

LEFT: The purple-blue flowers of borage (*Borago officinalis*), which droop from delicately hairy stems, are a beautiful garnish for salads and cooling summer drinks, and crystallized or fresh, they're a nice alternative to expensive candied violets. Dried in silica, they make pretty (though inedible) decorations for wreaths and other handicrafts. Borage is thought by some to be a good companion plant with a degree of natural pest repellent, so consider planting it among more susceptible plants.

RIGHT: The root of purple coneflower (*Echinacea purpurea*) has long been used in the treatment of fever and infection, and current research is investigating how it strengthens the immune system. A favorite plant for the perennial flower border, *Echinacea* usually flowers about three feet (90cm) off the ground with pink-to-purple rays surrounding a dramatic central cone. Of interest to those who enjoy their gardens primarily at twilight, a white form is available. The plant is native to North American prairies.

RIGHT: Garden sage (*Salvia officinalis*), historically thought to prolong life, is vital to the herb garden of any cook. The elongated, faintly downy, silvered foliage is very aromatic and essential in many poultry, meat, bread, and soup recipes. A tender perennial shrub, the plant typically grows two to two and a half feet (60–75cm) tall. Sage is handsome in combination with many other border and kitchen garden plants, and happily there is a wide selection from which to choose, among them purple sage, scarlet sage, variegated sage (with white and green; gold and green; or green, purple-pink, and white leaves), Mexican sage (*S. leucantha*), pineapple sage (*S. elegans*), and clary sage (*S. sclarea*). Give sage a sunny location with fast-draining soil.

LEFT: One way to control the exuberant nature of mint is to plant it in a container, to prevent it from spreading and crowding out its neighbors. Here, glossy leaves are in bright contrast to an old bucket. You have only to bruise mint foliage slightly to release the powerful aroma. A collection of easygoing mints might include lemon, apple, pineapple, and chocolate mint, in addition to the classic peppermint and spearmint.

ABOVE: This bright jumble was designed as an edible garden. Nasturtiums weave through a company of lettuce, salvia, and *Calendula* 'Orange King' and 'Neon'. Plant combinations are happiest when all the individuals share cultural preferences. These sun-lovers offer an arresting variety of foliage types.

OPPOSITE: A golden-leafed cultivar of marjoram (*Origanum vulgare* 'Aureum', also known as golden oregano) in a graceful terra-cotta pot highlights the meticulous caretaking of this potager. The potting mixture can be formulated to whatever the inhabitant of the pot likes best—in this case, a free-draining, somewhat sandy blend.

ABOVE LEFT: The yellow-green leaves of lemon balm (*Melissa officinalis*) hint at their uncannily lemony fragrance. Bees are keenly interested in the small, white flowers, hence another common name for the plant, bee balm. The toothed leaves are the basis for a famously soothing French infusion, and have been used in numerous medicinal preparations. Fresh lemon balm is delicious in dressings and stuffings, drinks cold and hot, soups, and fruit dishes.

ABOVE RIGHT: *Thymus doerfleri* fashions a creeping carpet of enthusiastic purplish blossoms. This wildly flowering ornamental is generally easygoing, and is happy when sited in a sunny, well-drained spot.

LEFT: This serene study in soft purples is composed of blue *Viola* and hardy catmint (*Nepeta faassenii*).

OPPOSITE: The fiery color of the hips and haws of numerous plants captures the attention of hungry wildlife. These make beautiful additions to such handicrafts as wreaths. The brilliant hips of *Rosa rugosa*, rich in Vitamin C, are sought for the making of an excellent jelly, and are delicious in teas and baked goods.

AN HERB FOR EVERY GARDEN

Whatever the situation in which you garden, herbs can play supporting or starring roles, as you choose. They offer myriad possibilities for naturalistic and formal gardens alike, and herbs can likewise work their magic in gardens of all sizes. The smallest corner is large enough for a garden. Window boxes and woodland paths, modest cottage gateways and imposing gravel courtyards, around birdbaths and by the seashore, all these are wonderful places to enjoy herbs. For the contrast they offer in texture, for their magnificent variety of foliage, flower, and fragrance, herbs belong in every garden.

ABOVE: Lady's mantle (Alchemilla mollis), purple sage, chives in full flower, and poppies create an exuberant little border that sits between a path of old brick and a wooden fence of soft green. Small though this growing area is, it will make a nice contribution to floral arrangements and in the kitchen.

OPPOSITE: A walled terrace offers a sheltered climate with the benefit of warmer temperatures. Steps positioned near the wall make it possible to arrange plants at various heights and change the garden picture on a whim, rather than relying entirely on the hope that the plants will grow into the desired effect.

LEFT: The gold-tinged lichen growing on this venerable stone bench is echoed in the variegated foliage of the shrub and in the diminutive herb garden at its feet. With its symmetry and tiny standard at its center, this minute garden is quite at home in its stately surroundings.

BELOW: This weathered stone trough is kept company by a host of terra-cotta pots of various sizes. Foxgloves call attention to the picturesque stone wall that marks the garden boundary.

OPPOSITE: A single strawberry pot is home to variegated nasturtiums, catmint, Johnny jump-ups, variegated thyme, and scented-leaf geraniums. An imaginative variety of plantings isn't limited by lack of space.

ABOVE: Thriving in the radiant heat from a stone wall, creeping Jenny, houseleek, scented-leaf geranium, mint, thyme, and purple sage are clustered to create a container garden. The individual plants provide different shades of green, ranging from tones of yellow-white through blue-green, to purple.

ABOVE: A romantic notion, this garden seat is planted with fragrant chamomile. The little plants are resilient enough to survive frequent visitation. Chamomile can be grown over footpaths, too, releasing wonderful scent with every step.

RIGHT: What thyme may lack in height, it more than makes up for in impact. With such luxuriant flowering as this, it can be relied on to glorify any sunny corner.

ABOVE: Less contained than it is punctuated by an iron fence, this planting gives the impression of a cottage garden. A path of lavender in shades of deep amethyst contrasts handsomely with the yellow stone of the house. The herb can be harvested judiciously from a border hedge of this generous size without spoiling the effect.

ABOVE: A garden such as this, with a strong sense of design and structure provided by paved paths and hedges, can be as enticing in winter as it is in summer; even in a harsher climate, without the pretty sight of the plants so fancifully frosted, the "bones" of this garden would ensure an interesting picture. Thoughtful pruning gives the trees their exquisite silhouettes, a natural foil to the formal style of this spacious, quiet refuge.

OPPOSITE: This seaside garden uses a natural rock formation as a "planter," an opportunity to improve the soil to the inhabitants' liking. Because wind off the ocean carries with it a good deal of salt, the most delicate of herbs should be reserved for more protected locations.

RIGHT: Window boxes, casual almost by definition, are ideal for patchwork plantings that bring together fruits, herbs, and ornamentals. This summer combination includes upright, mounding, and trailing plants.

BELOW: Include herbs in a wildlife garden. Many—such as alliums, roses, coneflowers, salvias, lavender, and nasturtiums—attract butterflies, hummingbirds, and bees. A diverse plant community makes an attractive habitat for many small creatures in search of food and shelter.

ABOVE: Where space is not at a premium, gardeners are free to include anything they desire. A paving of large, smooth pebbles makes harvesting from this garden a simple task even when rain has turned the soil to mud. Planning has made for easy access to each of these plant groupings.

ABOVE: A garden lavishly planted in front of the house is at once beautiful and practical. The herbs growing here are but a step from the doorway. With areas for strolling and for restful contemplation, this closely planted garden is also fairly drought-tolerant, without a water-guzzling lawn of high-maintenance grass.

Part Two

VINES AND CLIMBERS

INTRODUCTION

*M*ystery. Maturity. Opulence, abundance, and adventure. Vines and climbers can bring many moods to a landscape. These creeping, crawling, climbing, twining plants can give a garden new dimensions by adding height, depth, and romance.

Vines and climbers can serve as the backbone of a garden by adding structure to a developing landscape or revitalizing an older one.

Vines can be humble and undemanding, growing in the background and fulfilling the role of a framework for favorite plants. Or they can serve as featured plants by covering a trellis or arbor with fascinating foliage or beautiful blooms.

They can divide a landscape into outdoor rooms, giving special areas a feeeling of intimacy. Providing shade faster than a tree, covering ground more rapidly than grass, vines can also fill a space while you're waiting for slower plants to come into their own.

Vines and climbers seem to burst with energy. You can almost feel their inexorable growth as soon as you enter a garden where they live. Vines bring a sense of motion to the garden. They seem to spring to life as soon as they hit the ground, and always convey a feeling of growth barely under control.

So much of our gardening is done at ground level: we bend and stoop and crawl. Vines and climbers direct our vision upward; their foliage being at the gardener's eye level. When you're ready to move beyond simple beds and borders, it's time to move up to vines.

OPPOSITE: Climbers have their own seasons of glory in the sun. *Vitis Coignetiae* comes alive in streaming sunlight and, here, frames a fountain in a formal scene.

ABOVE: Sometimes vines are most valuable when they stretch out rather than up. Here, vinca serves as a backdrop to highlight a bright red azalea. The green carpet helps to knit the flowering plant to the stone path.

LEFT: When a light hand is called for, vines may be used to mimic or enhance natural conditions. This soft blanket of running cedar surrounding the base of a tree presents a clean, weedless look without seeming artificial.

ABOVE: Climbers need not be massive and intrusive to make a statement. Here, a simple vine wreath against a weathered fence creates a decorative addition.

OPPOSITE: Roses are at the top of most gardeners' lists of favorite climbing plants. At some point, nearly every gardener has dreamed of a rose-covered cottage. Here, rambling over the roof and sides of the cottage, the flowers perfume the air with their sweet fragrance.

LEFT: Mystery hangs like warm, thick air in this garden corner, where the light is softened by a profusion of vines both above and below. These vines serve to frame the formal fountain and focus attention on it.

OPPOSITE: Sometimes vines are asked to remain in the background and faithfully serve as accompaniment to surrounding garden plants and features. This trellis seems to be awaiting the growth of a vine, perhaps from the ivy climbing the nearby tree, adding a sense of expectation to the garden scene.

OPPOSITE: Gardeners often think of German ivy as a green screen that's easily ignored as it fades into the background. But in autumn, the ivy bursts into color. An awareness of the changing faces of vines and a readiness to combine them with surrounding colors allows the observant designer to create an eye-catching scene.

ABOVE: Some vines, such as wisteria, are coveted for their color. The spare architectural form of the vine and the airy clouds of bloom are light enough to let hardscape accents, like this window frame, shine through. Even unlikely color combinations work well with wisteria.

ABOVE: Virginia creeper and buttercup ivy have been given free rein to grow wild, bringing a feeling of age and enchantment to a corner of the garden. It may be for only a small spot in a new garden, but ivy, coupled with the artful placement of a garden artifact, adds a feeling of depth to the scene.

ABOVE: Light, airy, old-fashioned, and just plain pretty, sweet peas and runner beans on a trellis provide a focal point for the vegetable garden, giving it a more unique quality.

OPPOSITE: Like bright raindrops dripping down a wall, these vines add a sense of movement to the scene and draw the eye to the trough of alpine plants on the ground.

ABOVE: Tracing the outline of this wooden fence, these nasturtiums seem ready to embrace anyone who cares to stop and rest on the stone bench.

OPPOSITE: In the limited space of an urban patio, the vertical quality of vines provides the ability to create an interesting arrangement. The pot of 'Carnival de Nice' tulips adds a splash of color to the green backdrop. This composition, framed by the variegated leaves of the vine draped over the wall, can be enjoyed indoors or out.

ABOVE: Some vining plants, such as wisteria, can be trained as standards that do not need any support. They add a sense of seclusion to the surrounding garden.

OPPOSITE: Hanging like jewels from a bracelet, golden laburnum and purple wisteria add height and depth to this garden bed.

DESIGNING WITH VINES AND CLIMBERS

*S*ooner or later, faced with a bare wall, a boring lawn, or a young garden that's slow to mature, every gardener recognizes the appeal of vines and climbers. They're among the most versatile of all garden plants. It would be difficult to find another plant that would work as hard or as fast to transform a landscape.

Vines and climbers can match any mood you wish to create in the garden. The dignified and stately look of an ivy-covered hall or the bright and cheery country feel of morning glories on a garden fence are just two examples of the effective uses of vines.

When considering the look you desire for your garden, give a little thought to vines. Do you need a vertical accent or a splash of color to draw the eye? You might desire an arbor covered with clematis. Do you need to soften a fence that surrounds a vegetable garden? Sow morning glories or nasturtiums. Is your lawn growing old and hard to maintain? Consider a lamium or pachysandra corner to reduce the size of your lawn. Perhaps you want to create a secluded, mysterious spot in the corner of the garden. Ivy will do the trick quickly.

Always keep in mind the effect you're after. If you want an airy, bright feel, use annual flowering vines. To extend the garden season, choose evergreen perennial vines. Or try combining a few different vines. Whatever you choose, you're sure to find that your garden can be improved by adding the vertical accents of vines and climbers.

OPPOSITE: An arbor at a lawn's edge is an inviting spot to stop and survey the garden. These informal, fast-growing hops spilling over the arbor provide a natural, untamed feeling, matching the catmint planting below.

ABOVE: A wooden door and an adobe wall may seem stark and uninviting, but as ivy crawls over the hard surface, it softens the scene and makes the entry seem more approachable.

ABOVE: Climbers and creepers can be combined in a landscape for a lush effect. Billowing jasmine on an arbor seems to rise on the horizon like a cloud from a sea of green ivy.

RIGHT: All too often patios are overexposed and thus seem uninviting. A simple arbor of roses provides a sense of security and enclosure to this space, making it a more welcoming place to spend a summer afternoon.

OPPOSITE: Sometimes slight and delicate vines, such as these runner beans, are the perfect touch. Here, they allow the beauty of the trellis to show through.

OPPOSITE: It's a rare landscape that entices the visitor to look up; so much of our time in the garden is spent gazing downward. Plants that guide our vision and our spirits upward, such as this wisteria on a pergola, feel especially refreshing and rich.

LEFT: Getting the most from vines requires planning and some patience. Consider the structure and material that the plant will grow against. Do you want contrast or harmony? A white blooming hydrangea goes well with most supporting colors. Pruned sparingly, it can't help but be noticed and appreciated.

ABOVE: Gardens, especially new ones, can sometimes seem too flat and one-dimensional. But an arbor covered with a fast-growing vine, such as clematis, offers an entirely new dimension.

ABOVE: With its supple stems, ivy can be trained to take the shape of any garden and its accents. This vine will eagerly grow to cover a sphere with just a bit of tending.

RIGHT: Color is key to any garden. Sometimes subdued shades are called for. At other times and in other places, brighter and bolder colors are better. A blazing trumpet vine calls attention to this courtyard.

OPPOSITE: An entryway is the first place that a vine can make an impact. The first decision for the gardener is whether to choose a vine that climbs or trails. Even in the dark, the scent of this trailing jasmine will draw the visitor to the gate.

ABOVE: Repetition and rhythm are easily incorporated when designing with vines. Elegant climbing roses frame a simple door; the pattern is then repeated on the window beside it.

RIGHT: Climbing plants can add a sense of order to lush and jumbled plantings. Standing like bookends, these roses frame the plantings and draw the eye upward. At the same time, they're trained to conform to the pattern on the brick wall.

ABOVE: When it comes to climbing plants, there are few that are as versatile and as full of feeling as roses. Old-fashioned climbers can add a dash of color to a rustic scene. Even if they're newly planted, they bring to mind abandoned wild plantings.

RIGHT: A bower of wisteria can punctuate a garden path and provide a welcome relief from the summer sun.

LEFT: Vibrant when in full bloom, jasmine seems to take on many new qualities. Here, it appears as a welcoming guest at this patio table where the vine's sweet scent perfumes the air.

ABOVE: English ivy is often used as a rampant cover, left to grow eagerly over all it encounters. For a more elegant look, keep ivy's growth in check with careful pruning, and it will follow and echo the shape of a trellis or arbor.

ABOVE: Width and breadth are as important as height when designing with vines. Here, roses are kept within boundaries to remain in the same scale as the bench—and perfume without being overwhelming. Visitors who stop to rest here will be embraced by the roses' beauty.

LEFT: Sometimes a simple coverlet of green is all that's called for. Ivy adds a sense of enchantment to the corner of this garden.

ABOVE: We often think of ivy as a mass, a plant best left to cover vast, blank areas. But it can also serve as a rich green accent in an off-season window box.

ABOVE: Even when ivy is put to work on a common task, such as covering a brick wall, its effect can be heightened by such accessories as these delicate shutters and simple window box.

RIGHT: Clematis is a garden favorite, renowned for its abundant, rich blooms, delicate foliage, and genteel climbing habits. Light and airy, it's best used to emphasize the frame on which it grows.

PROBLEM-SOLVING VINES

*W*e use flowers, shrubs, and trees as bright splashes of paint on our landscape canvases. We may plant and feed and fuss over them, but they are only a small part of the picture. For best presentation they need only a well-thought-out background. But too often the space around and between annuals and perennials is blank canvas, most likely a long, dull stretch of labor-intensive lawn. Creeping ground covers can add a more exciting texture and tone to the overall picture.

Vines don't have to grow upward to enhance a yard. Sometimes their horizontal nature is just as welcome in a garden. There are many vines that are at their best when they're allowed room to roam. Planted in corners, they'll soften the edges of the lawn. They can also provide a transition between that patch of grass and more wild areas. Grown around a deck, vines can impart a look that turf cannot.

Versatile ground covers bring many looks to a landscape. They can be as well behaved and understated as pachysandra or as stately as ivy. They can be as wild as honeysuckle, evoking the feeling of an abandoned estate.

Creeping vines are, as a rule, undemanding. Growing thick and running fast and far, they require little care.

OPPOSITE: Bright yellow creeping Jenny finds a more subdued mate in the pink-flowered sedum. Together they blanket the ground with color, which will last throughout the season.

ABOVE: As vigorous as a weed, Hall's honeysuckle will climb, creep, and trail as long as it is allowed. It can be used to cover ground, structures, or any material that's best hidden.

ABOVE: What do you turn to when you need cover in a hurry? The common morning glory. Nothing grows faster to form a deep carpet of fresh green foliage. And nothing compares to its cheery blooms, either.

RIGHT: A rampant grower, honeysuckle will cover everything in its path, forming a thicket that smothers weeds. The variety 'Dropmore Scarlet' is favored for its bright red flowers that persist from early summer into late autumn.

ABOVE: It grows fast to cover the ground in great waves of white-spotted dark green leaves. It erupts into blue flowers that fade to pink. It thrives north or south, in sunlight or light shade. All these characteristics make Bethlehem sage one of the best ground covers around.

ABOVE: There's no ground cover more common than pachysandra, but freed from its usual placement—in the circle surrounding the base of a tree—and left to roam over an expansive area, pachysandra can add an element of elegance to the landscape.

RIGHT: Sometimes a mound of flowers is the key to a successful landscape. Abundant with blooms, clematis can easily fill that role.

OPPOSITE: A ground cover need not exist only as a uniform sea of green. Mixing plants adds interest and excitement. Here, saxifrage, lamium, and euphorbia are combined for a striking effect.

OPPOSITE: Woodbine, with its stately stems and refined foliage, is a good choice to cover gates, fences, and walls. It takes on an interesting look through the seasons as small green flowers give way to dark berries and bright autumn foliage.

LEFT: Some ground covers are made for the shade. Lamium, with its silver leaves and clusters of delicate flowers, prefers to grow where the soil is moist and the sunlight is dim.

ABOVE: Versatility is one of the strengths of common ivy. Gardeners can use it in many different ways, such as allowing it to creep and flow down a set of stone steps.

LEFT: Climbing roses grow fast and bloom profusely, and many offer a delightful scent, making them a perfect choice for covering walls and fences.

OPPOSITE: It's sometimes hard to understand the obscurity of porcelain *Ampelopsis.* This deciduous perennial grows fast and strong with handsome bright leaves and makes a good arbor ornament. In late summer and autumn, it produces clusters of bird-attracting berries of many colors.

LEFT: The bright bark of a eucalyptus tree seems even richer when contrasted with a climbing blanket of ivy. The vine also serves to keep the ground free of weeds and undesirable plants.

OPPOSITE: A planter filled with bright annuals could be lost against a plain brick background. But a wall of ivy plays the perfect supporting role, allowing the flowering plants to shine.

FAST EFFECTS WITH ANNUAL VINES AND CLIMBERS

They may not grow quite as fast as Jack's beanstalk, but annual vines can make fast magic in the landscape. Sown in spring, the plants seem to burst from the soil and climb upward without pause. In the process they'll quickly transform a garden spot with their lush foliage and vibrant blooms.

Does your vegetable garden seem a bit dull? A few bright-flowered ornamental beans clambering up a tepee will take care of that. Want to dress up that front fence? A few morning glories twining through the pickets will transform the scene. Waiting for shrubs, trees, or a hedge to fill in? You can put annual vines to work as part-time scene stealers.

In just a weekend you can begin a new look for a garden spot. Erect a simple trellis and sow a few seeds, and you're on your way to a new dimension in gardening.

Annual vines and climbers are growth personified. These simple, unassuming plants convey their own special playfulness and free nature. Covering walls and fences or climbing up trellises, they speak of sunny summer days, bright cottage gardens, and country farmhouses.

OPPOSITE: If provided with a foothold, nasturtiums will climb by twisting their leaf stems around a trellis, fence, wire, or wall. The edible flowers add a peppery flavor to salads.

ABOVE: It's hard to beat nasturtiums for fast cover and rich colors. The plants bring an old-fashioned look to the edge of a flower or vegetable garden that never goes out of favor.

LEFT: Known as clock vine for its bright, orange faces, *Thunbergia* brings a lush tropical look to a hanging planter, window box, or garden bed. This Mexican native grows fast from seed and thrives in the sun.

ABOVE: Vegetables that are equally at home in the flower garden or clambering up a porch post, scarlet runner beans offer rich, bright colors on delicate, quick-twining vines.

ABOVE: It may be their deep, pure colors of violet, white, and pink, or perhaps it's their petals' velvety look or fresh green leaves. Maybe it's the speed with which they grow, or the memories of simple gardens they inspire. Whatever the reason, morning glories never go out of fashion as a climbing vine for a fence or post.

RIGHT: Morning glory vines may reach up to ten feet (3m) in length in a single season. Just sow them in place in a sunny location and they'll find a way to climb into the spotlight.

ABOVE: The common nasturtium has an exotic relative that's rarely seen in gardens: the canary creeper. Though its flowers are smaller and always bright yellow, its foliage is more intriguing than that of the common nasturtium. It climbs more readily as well.

RIGHT: Hops are bound to attract attention and inspire comments from garden visitors. These rampant growers produce intriguing seed pods from which beer is made.

OPPOSITE: One of the best ways to beautify a vegetable planting is with a tepee of runner beans. The variety 'White Achievement' grows into a solid mass of foliage and blooms with delightful white flowers in midsummer.

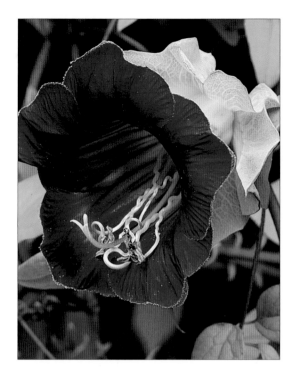

OPPOSITE: Flame flower is another nasturtium relative and has electrifying red blooms. Though perennial in warm areas, it's often grown as an annual where the weather is cool.

ABOVE: The cup and saucer vine offers large purple and green or white flowers on a fast-growing vine that may reach up to twenty-five feet (7.6m) in a single season. This Mexican native can be sown in a sunny location and allowed to climb over a fence or trellis.

RIGHT: When the talk is of charming, old-fashioned flowers, sweet peas usually head the list. They're known for their wide variety of colors and delightful fragrance.

PERMANENCE FROM PERENNIAL VINES

*P*erennial vines and climbers add permanence and stateliness to the landscape. With their strong forms, rich textures, and elegant blooms, perennial vines can enliven a wall or an arbor. Above all else, they convey the feeling of energetic growth. Indeed, they make a landscape come alive with their ambition. Covering a wall or climbing relentlessly up an arbor or a pergola, they seem to say that nature will not be subdued.

A garden can be built around perennial vines and climbers. If you plant them in a good spot, they'll be there from year to year, adding their own elegant tone to the garden. Many offer exotic flowers in deep colors and appealing shapes. Others remain attractive through all four seasons, offering autumn color or having bright green foliage through the bleak winter months.

The features of perennial vines are nearly endless. Many provide exotic flowers that attract butterflies and hummingbirds, or grow gnarled strong trunks that offer shelter to birds.

Perennial vines are perfect for hefty arbors, classic pergolas, porches, and walls. These climbers can hold their own against large structures, reducing the hardscape of the landscape to an appealing scale.

OPPOSITE: Wisteria provides a touch of southern elegance far into northern areas. The rich purple or white flowers appear early in spring, releasing their seductive fragrance far and wide.

ABOVE: At first glance you might not guess that actinidia is a close relative of the plant that bears kiwi fruit. This ornamental kiwi unfurls its leaves in spring with an unlikely combination of white, pink, and green. If both male and female plants are present, they will also produce small, edible fruit.

ABOVE: Five-leaf akebia offers nearly everything a gardener could want. Its woody vines, covered with delicate foliage, produce sweet-smelling flowers in spring. It can also find a place in the food garden as it grows smalls clusters of handsome edible fruit. Growing to thirty feet (9.1m), akebia can be planted to climb a trellis or ramble over the ground.

RIGHT: Star jasmine is tougher than it looks. Its delicate white flowers and delightful scent belie its aggressive nature and tough demeanor. It's a good choice for covering banks and clambering up walls.

OPPOSITE: Clematis is often the first choice for a perennial climber, and a good choice it is. This herbaceous vine grows rapidly in spring from a moist, shady site, with large, luxurious blooms exploding into the sunlight. Clematis will climb a lamppost, cover a roof, or spread over a bank without fuss.

OPPOSITE: The crimson glory vine, a common grape relative, is at its best in autumn. That's when the foliage turns a fiery red and lights up the landscape.

LEFT: Ivy is the strong, silent type in the landscape. It grows fast and does all that is required without complaint. Ivy is often over-looked, but variegated varieties such as *Hedera colchica* 'Sulpherheart' are more noticeable.

ABOVE: A single purple wisteria flower cluster, reaching up to twenty inches (50.8cm) in length, is a thing of beauty in itself. A mature vine covered with blooms can take one's breath away.

ABOVE: An evergreen in warm areas such as Florida, the passion flower is one of the more dramatic flowering vines. Fast-growing and vigorous, the plant produces sweetly scented flowers that attract butterflies.

RIGHT: Available in many shapes, sizes, and colors, Italian clematis 'Abundance' is known for its rapid growth and delicate hanging, pinkish red flowers that appear in late summer.

ABOVE: Porcelain *Ampelopsis* is known for its bright berries of blue, green, purple, and pink. They appear in autumn on beautiful, strong plants.

OPPOSITE: Though they won't climb without assistance, roses are among the most popular choices for covering walls and fences. 'Climbing Peace' may be the most renowned of gardeners' favorites. With just a little help, these roses will gladly grow skyward.

ABOVE: Porches are where you'll normally find Dutchman's-pipe. The twining vines quickly climb any available support, while the huge, kidney-shaped leaves provide deep shade. In late spring, small, brown, pipe-shaped flowers appear.

RIGHT: Even the common grape vine can play a leading role as a climber in the ornamental garden. Its lush foliage turns a deep red as autumn approaches.

ABOVE: The foliage is the most popular characteristic of ivy. Always green, it shines in seasons long after other climbers and vines have given up the ghost. Ivy keeps the garden alive all through the year.

RIGHT: The climbing hydrangea is a stately plant in any setting. Its small, white, beautifully fragrant flowers cover the strong vines of this plant in spring and early summer.

Part Three
ROSE GARDENS

INTRODUCTION

For its lore, mystique, and romance, the rose stands alone. Planting a rose introduces its rich heritage to your landscape, and we recall its storied past every time we glimpse its vibrant beauty or inhale its delicate fragrance. Countless poems have been written about the rose; wars have been fought over it; and it's been an ingredient in the formulas of medieval alchemists. More than any other flower we can plant, the rose represents love and affection. It truly embodies the perfection of nature.

With its flawless flower, its tantalizing fragrance, and its classic form, a rose can transform a garden. Whether alone in a long formal bed, mixed with perennials in a border, or climbing a porch, roses always seem to fit your landscape—and your desires.

Roses freely contribute their majesty to a garden. All eyes are drawn to them when they are in bloom. But they are capable of surprising, too. They can be modest like the simple, humble blooms of New England shining roses (Rosa nitida). They can be as informal as the glossy foliage and bright hips of rugosa roses (Rosa rugosa). Or they can display the exuberance of wild rambling roses. However you choose to use them, roses are sure to serve as the crowning touch in your garden.

ABOVE: It's easy to get lost in the perfect bloom of a rose. Whether the flowers are single and simplicity itself or double and full—like those of this floribunda, 'Margaret Merril'—rose blossoms, pure and fragrant, add enchantment to any garden scene.

OPPOSITE: Roses bring a feeling of luxury to the landscape. Many rose classes offer a profusion of blooms on thick, full bushes that add drama to a vast landscape or even to just the corner of a bed. Here, the shrub rose 'Constance Spry' covers itself with fragrant pink blooms in high summer.

ABOVE: For all their majesty, roses fit in gracefully with other flowering and foliage plants, serving here as an exclamation point in a border of herbaceous perennials. The white blooms of the shrub rose 'Nevada' appear in midsummer and continue to rebloom until autumn.

LEFT: A rosebush is the ultimate enticement. The pure pink blooms of the gallica rose 'Versicolor' anchor a seating area and make it even more inviting. Gallica roses, first grown by the Romans, exude a delicious fragrance that's difficult to resist.

ABOVE: Asked to imagine a single rose, most of us would picture the delicately folded blossom of a hybrid tea. In truth, hybrid teas are fairly recent introductions to the world of roses. But every garden should have at least one, to add "rose-ness" to the landscape and elegance to the home as a cut flower.

RIGHT: There are so many classes and cultivars of roses, and the plants and blooms occur in such an assortment of forms and hues, that it's easy to find an ideal cultivar for any type of surroundings. This shrub rose seems perfectly at home adorning the porch of a rustic cottage.

ABOVE: Like a living tapestry, the climbing rose 'Constance Spry' hangs over a brick wall. Its intoxicating scent drifts over a classic white bench, creating a nearly irresistible resting spot.

OPPOSITE: Hundreds of years of breeding have given birth to increasingly complex roses, but the plant's ancient roots have not been forgotten. A species rose such as *Rosa glauca* is a welcome addition to the landscape for its simple, starlike flower and striking, blue-gray foliage.

ABOVE: Roses are so commanding that all it takes is a single bloom to lift the landscape out of the ordinary. The exquisitely striped pink-and-white floribunda 'Peppermint Twist' offers a scintillating splash of color.

LEFT: Something unusual happened in the breeding of hybrid teas. Plants occasionally threw up sports—mutant plants with new characteristics. Such a sport was the origin of the climbing rose, which allows us to enjoy the prolific blooms of the hybrid teas in vertical spaces.

ABOVE: The rediscovery of antique roses makes one wonder why they were ever neglected. Old roses, such as this 'Rosa Mundi', contribute a feeling of timelessness to the formal garden.

ABOVE: Sometimes roses are most appreciated when they are allowed to dominate, with just a bit of help from a supporting cast. The lanky growth of Bourbon roses can be complemented with an underplanting of simple flowers such as pansies.

LEFT: As if the fantastic blooms, enchanting fragrance, regal foliage, and stunning form of roses were not enough, many offer an autumn show of glossy hips. This fruit—popular in teas, jams, and jellies—endures to decorate the winter landscape.

ABOVE: Roses rise to the occasion in this formal island bed. Climbing varieties, such as 'Madame Caroline Testout', will readily clamber up a support, adding height and color to the garden.

ABOVE: Fairy tales and storybooks come to mind as the visitor approaches this scene. The climbing rose, intertwined with white-flowering clematis, is the final magical touch.

ABOVE: Roses can serve as a centerpiece or they can contribute their enchantment from afar. A house in the distance is honored by the 'Morning Jewel' rose that frames a view of it.

ABOVE: At home in the cottage garden, the formal border, or the wild landscape, roses are never too refined to fit into a garden. 'Scarlet Fire', a recently introduced shrub rose, manages to combine elegance with a casual air.

ABOVE: Floating like a cloud, the crystalline blooms of 'Iceberg' roses draw the eye toward the focal point of the garden, a magnificent urn filled with geraniums. While not technically the central players in this lush garden, the roses serve as a lovely frame for the picture.

OPPOSITE: The wise gardener considers form and color when combining roses with other plants. These tall, spiky delphiniums are emphasized by the cascade of pale roses in the background.

SOCIABLE CLIMBERS

*I*t almost seems too much to ask: a cascade of flawless flowers in intricate forms and bright colors spilling over a fence or climbing up a wall, releasing their alluring scent into the evening air. But climbing roses bring that dream within reach of every gardener.

Roses are at their most dramatic when they're growing up and over a support. Climbing and rambling roses evoke the feeling of antiquity as they scale an arbor, clamber over a fence, or cover a brick building.

In these plants you can sense the wild nature of early roses. They carry a sense of abandon into the garden as vigorous canes lift the flowers to eye level and beyond, displaying the glorious flowers and allowing their scent to tumble on the wind.

Another benefit of climbing roses: these exuberant plants grow fast, filling a garden with sheer vitality. And they do it without complaint. All that's required is an annual pruning to remove old and damaged canes, and winter protection in cold areas.

OPPOSITE: Though roses have no tendrils to pull themselves up a brick wall, a thin wire provides enough support. The wire seems to disappear behind the shiny green foliage and bright blooms of a climbing rose such as 'Celine Forrestier'.

RIGHT: A landscape can be created with climbing roses as the focal point. Two climbing roses, 'Helen Knight' and 'Madame Alfred Carriere', meet above a leaded glass window. A bed of pale yellow irises in the foreground adds the dimension of contrasting flower form to the scene.

ABOVE: What goes up can also come down. Climbing roses appear most romantic when they are allowed to hang and trail gracefully. Here, 'Alister Stella Grey' lends atmosphere to a latticed garden bench.

OPPOSITE: Climbing roses are often at their best when seen from below. Framed by a bright blue sky, the pale pink climber 'New Dawn' comes alive. Just two of these vigorous plants will quickly cover a trellis.

ABOVE: A 'Queen of Denmark' rose floats whimsically over a bench. Just a single plant clambering up an arbor softens the hard edges of the landscape and showers the sitting area with its sweet scent.

LEFT: Roses add grace and grandeur to any garden scene. As 'Lady Hillingdon' scrambles over an arched gate, it refreshes the landscape. Climbing roses are the focal point of this scene, rising above the clipped box in an urn and hostas in the distance.

ABOVE: Roses are not solitary creatures. They'll happily combine with many other forms of garden flowers and foliage. Here, the roses 'Minnehaha' and 'Aloha' prove perfect companions for clematis and campanula.

LEFT: Roses can own a landscape. An entire pergola in this English garden is given over to 'Rambling Rector' rose, adding an aura of lushness to the well-manicured lawn.

ABOVE: All roses offer a rainbow of colors, but the varied class of climbing and rambling roses offers a wide selection of foliage and flower forms as well. 'American Pillar', for instance, is covered with clusters of tiny flowers.

ABOVE: By nature, climbing and rambling roses invite admiration from a distance. But step in for a closer look at *Rosa* 'Verschuren', the Lambook rose—each flower inspires awe with its delicate, ruffled bloom.

RIGHT: 'Paul's Scarlet' covers a pergola with rich red blooms in midsummer. Though it blossoms only once a season, its semidouble bloom blankets the foliage. This variety also makes a fine shrub rose if pruned regularly.

ABOVE: No matter what fills the surrounding garden, a rose pergola always serves as the ultimate destination. It draws us to bask in the color and scent of the flowers that drape it. This stately wood and brick pergola is decked with masses of 'Aloha', 'Sanders White', and 'Compassion'.

ABOVE: A rustic pergola serves as a perfect support for a collection of climbing roses. It lifts the striking blooms of 'Bleu Magenta'—one of the more unusual climbers—above the surrounding perennials. Here, the bluish red rose is flanked by companion climbers 'Wedding Day' and 'Botany Bay'.

LEFT: Climbing roses do have one shortcoming—some have a short bloom time. But there's an easy and elegant fix: fill in the blanks with a companionable climber like this large-flowered purple clematis.

ABOVE: Though it is a tender plant and requires some pampering, yellow Lady Banks' rose (*Rosa banksiae* var. *lutea*) is well worth the trouble. Its small flowers cover the vine with a dazzling display of blooms in early spring.

OPPOSITE: Climbing roses almost always represent a riot of disorganized bloom and foliage. Here, a border of well-tended lavender along a stone path balances the exuberant blooms with order and definition.

ABOVE: Rambling roses offer even more vigorous growth than their cousins, the climbers. Ramblers have more flexible canes, a trait that allows the plants to be used as groundcovers. Or, like this 'Tausendschon', ramblers may be trained to scramble over a wall.

ABOVE: Sometimes even roses that are not classed as climbers can be persuaded to adopt a rambling habit. 'The Fairy' is an exceedingly vigorous shrub rose that shines when it is left to scurry over a split rail fence. As a bonus, it's hardier than most climbers.

OPPOSITE: Is there anything in the world of horticulture that says "welcome" better than climbing roses adorning a door? A 'Penelope' rose lends an inviting softness to this somewhat austere dooryard.

THE REST OF THE ROSES

What's in a name? Plenty. A rose by any other name might smell as sweet, but when it comes to planning and planting the landscape, it helps to understand the nomenclature of roses. That might seem an impossible task to the beginner. There are scores of different classes of roses, from the ancient Rosa chinensis, *or China roses, to the modern shrub roses. Over centuries of breeding the lines have blurred until even experienced rosarians argue over them.*

In general, though, each class has its own characteristics and requirements. A basic familiarity with these classes and the cultivars within them can help you choose the right roses for your situation.

In time you can learn the subtleties of the rose, but what's most important is to choose a look you like, whether it's the simple single bloom of a wild rose or the elaborate swirl of a hybrid tea. First choose the rose that takes your breath away—the one that seems to have been bred for your garden and your sensibility—and then take the time to learn about it.

ABOVE: Modern roses, sometimes called modern crosses, combine the best of the old and the new, blurring the distinctions between the lines. The English rose is a new category. Its most famous breeder is David Austin, and a type has been named after him. David Austin roses are known for their hardiness, fragrance, and double flowers in pastel hues. 'Graham Thomas', the first yellow English rose, was one of Austin's creations.

OPPOSITE: Shrub roses encompass many classes, both old and new. All of them are welcome in the garden for their robust habit, and flowers may be once- or repeat-blooming. 'Pink Meidiland' has striking pink blossoms with white eyes, and blooms in both spring and autumn. This hardy and disease-resistant rose grows rapidly, topping off at four feet (1.2m).

ABOVE: A specialized form of the modern shrub rose, the hybrid musk is a wonder. The plant is rangy and rambling, best when combined with other plants in a mixed bed or border, but the flowers are refined. Blooming in delicate pastel shades, blossoms usually turn white as they fade. 'Buff Beauty' is a prolific repeat-bloomer that is constantly covered with roses in all stages of flowering.

ABOVE: When it comes to blooms, there's no rose that can surpasses the elegant, perfect, folded-petal form of the hybrid tea. And red 'Christian Dior' is the epitome of the hybrid tea rose.

OPPOSITE: Musk roses also come in a rambler form that makes a good addition to the informal cottage garden. 'Paul's Himalayan Musk Rambler' sports a pink blush on its glistening white blooms.

ABOVE: The multiflora rose, now naturalized throughout the United States, is native to China. Its origin gives a clue to its vigor and hardiness. As persistent as a weed—in fact it has been declared a weed in some areas—it produces abundant bright white blooms that are held in large, tight clusters.

ABOVE: Damask roses are among the most honored of old types. They first adorned the pleasure gardens of ancient Persia, and were later brought to Europe by the crusaders. 'Leda' is a very fragrant cultivar that it is winter hardy as well as virtually disease-free.

ABOVE: The multiflora species has been utilized as a parent for floribunda, polyantha, and musk roses, as well as for hybrid multifloras. 'Veilchenblau' is one of the more spectacular of the multiflora hybrids. It produces just a single flush of blooms in midseason, but the flowers cover this twelve-foot rambler (3.6m) with rich color, while exuding the scent of apples.

185

ABOVE: The Noisette class of roses was developed in the nineteenth century in South Carolina, and was named after their breeder, Philippe Noisette. They became a sensation for their repeat bloom and for their attractive clusters of clove-scented flowers. The Noisettes fell out of favor nearly one hundred years ago, but cultivars such as 'Crepuscule' are leading the class in a comeback.

ABOVE: Born of rambling parents, the polyanthas are tough and independent, requiring minimal care. They flower freely with little or no pruning. 'Ellen Poulsen' produces masses of clear pink blooms on a short bush.

ABOVE: 'Baronne Prevost' is a rose beyond reproach. Its refined, deeply scrolled blossoms, in shades of pale to deep pink, exude a rich, classic rose fragrance. And unlike its hybrid perpetual kin, the bush is vigorous and attractive.

LEFT: The origin of the miniature rose is shrouded in mystery, but there's no question about its utility. True miniatures, such as this creamy orange 'Chrissy', are scaled-down roses in bloom, leaf, and plant form. They're perfect for pots or window boxes, or as low border plants along a sunny path.

ABOVE: Growing a 'Caribbean' rose is like capturing the most spectacular sunset for your garden. The textured orange blooms adorn a strong bush, typical of its grandiflora class.

ABOVE: For those rosarians who like their flowers simple, 'Encore' is a perfect choice. This charming floribunda produces masses of blooms in a light pink blush.

ABOVE: The grandiflora is a relatively new class of roses, developed from floribunda stock in the 1950s. Roses in this family are characterized by clusters of flowers on towering bushes, though 'White Lightnin' is one of the smaller examples of the class.

ABOVE: Floribunda roses live up to their ambitious name. Derived from a fortuitous cross between ramblers and polyanthas, floribundas produce seemingly impossible masses of flowers. The bushes are also hardier and more disease resistant than those of hybrid teas. 'Golden Fleece' offers lush, bright yellow blooms.

ABOVE: The Bourbons seem to be almost perfect roses. Insistent repeat-bloomers, they flower prolifically through summer until the first frost. And what blooms! Complex, many-layered, and delicate, in shades of pink—like this 'Zephirine Drouhin'—the plants are vigorous, disease resistant, and winter hardy. They're wonderful along a walk, where their fragrance perfumes the air.

RIGHT: You'll find the rugosa rose growing wild along the seashore, as tough and vigorous as a weed. This rose's thick, hairy foliage and bright, single, fragrant blooms fit perfectly into the natural or casual garden. In fact it'll grow just about anywhere, dressing the garden with festive blooms in summer and colorful round hips in autumn.

ABOVE: The China rose, *Rosa chinensis*, is the parent of many of our modern roses, and has brought the enviable quality of repeat blooming to many cultivars. Though the blooms of many China roses are simple, almost dull compared with the complex flower forms other roses, the rich, pink blooms of *R. chinensis mutabilis* look like delicate butterflies at rest.

LEFT: There's been a boom in the breeding of modern roses, which has given rise to a whole new class, the David Austin roses. Named after their creator, the Austins are fine shrub roses, known for their hardy bushes, repeat blooms, and fragrant flowers. 'Prospero' is a fine example.

ROSES AND THE COMPANY THEY KEEP

*W*e think of roses as the royalty of the garden. True enough, over centuries of cultivation, they've earned a singular position in the landscape. Roses are strong enough to stand alone in the garden. But, because many do not bloom all season, they lend themselves well to integration with other types of plants.

Fortunately, roses are happy to share the stage. They will make themselves at home in the formal border, and they'll mix with an understory of annuals or a background of shrubs. Climbing roses or ramblers can serve as an exciting background for any type of plant. The rose's versatility is among its most unappreciated qualities.

The range of bloom colors, too, makes the rose a gardener's dream. From pale peaches and pinks to cool yellows to fiery reds and oranges—and even a few blues—there's sure to be a rose that matches your garden's color scheme.

OPPOSITE: Climbing roses might look sparse against a brick wall or may appear bare when flowers fade, but the tall flower spikes of foxglove help to fill in any empty spaces.

RIGHT: A four-foot (1.2m)-tall 'Iceberg' rosebush serves as a focal point in this garden. Its glowing white blooms give the eye an area of focus between the trees in the background and the herbaceous perennials in the foreground. A bamboo plant helps to ease the transition in height.

ABOVE: The bare stems of the climbing 'Ferdinand de Lesseps' rose are hidden by exuberant stalks of *Penstemon digitalis* in this border garden. The airy white penstemon help to sustain the illusion that the roses are floating against the brick.

LEFT: Companion plants for a rose garden should be chosen with their blooming seasons in mind. Bright yellow lily-flowered tulips are a perfect complement to the early-blooming 'Hugonis' rose in the background. The sweet blue blossoms of forget-me-nots round out this garden picture.

OPPOSITE: In some plantings, roses are at their best when they're allowed to play a supporting role. A single 'Buff Beauty' bush at the edge of this bed offers a unifying color element to the delphinium and lysimachia.

ABOVE: Roses don't have to be aloof in the garden. Their majesty is evident even when surrounded by other plants. A 'Camaieux' rose peeks through the bright blooms of *Stachys macrantha* and red valerian.

LEFT: Tall, lanky roses such as the alba 'Queen of Denmark' are at their best when surrounded by lofty garden plants. Here, 'Pink Beauty' tiger lily, *Phlomis italica*, and wallflower lend their enthusiastic presence.

ABOVE: Companion plants don't have to conform to the standard set by roses in order to work well. These small potted violas and alyssums make perfect partners for 'Cecile Brunner'. The rose seems to be bending in a friendly gesture to greet the diminutive flowers.

ABOVE: A simple combination in a small bed can heighten the magical effect of roses. This modest planting features height and depth with lavender, orange lilies, and the spectacular hybrid tea rose 'Tanzenroh'.

ABOVE: Roses can serve as an elegant filler in a bed or border. 'Compte de Chambord' and 'Veilchenblau' close the gaps and soften the edges of a pergola that is surrounded by a planting of honeysuckle, delphiniums, and catmint.

RIGHT: Pay attention to the harmony of colors when planning a garden around roses. Complementary colors work best, as when 'Fritz Nobis', a light pink rose, grows alongside purple berberis.

198

ABOVE: A sprawling pearly rose serves admirably to hold together the divergent plants—including lilies and hostas—in this white garden. When viewed at night the white blooms will seem to shimmer and glow in the moonlight.

ABOVE: Maybe all roads lead to Rome, but in some gardens, all plants lead to the rose. Purple geraniums and *Acanthus spinosus* set the stage for the daring red of a 'Charles de Mills' rose.

ABOVE: Roses will welcome other climbers. A careful and well-considered combination adds luster to their presence. Here, the rose 'Zephirine Drouhin' shares a trellis with *Clematis niobe.*

ABOVE: An 'American Pillar' rose adds elegance and order to a riotous border, rising up above the campanula, hollyhocks, phlox, and other plants. Heavy paving stones come to the aid of the roses in keeping this garden on the straight and narrow.

RIGHT: Shrub roses can occasionally appear severe and formal, a habit that may make them seem out of place in a naturalistic garden. But a good plant marriage shows their casual side. Here, wild columbine mixes well with the rose 'Greuss an Teplitz'.

ABOVE: A block of plants in a single color can serve to frame and draw attention to a prize rosebush. The 'Angel Blush' rose campion, with its small white flowers and gray-green leaves, is clearly a supporting player to the 'Ispahan' rose in this garden.

ABOVE: An occasional unexpected combination can be a hit in the well-planned garden. Roses usually cohabit with common temperate plants, but a gallica rose planted here with Mediterranean euphorbia is a sure winner.

ABOVE: This gardener has gone to great lengths to design a planting that highlights the roses. The strong lines of fountain grass serve as a perfect backdrop for 'The Fairy' rose, while a lamb's ears in the foreground offers contrasting color, shape, and texture.

RIGHT: Roses are true chameleons in the garden. Here, a planting with modest daisies reveals the humble side of roses.

A ROSE FOR ANY OTHER PLACE

*W*e've all seen the classic rose garden, with row after row of neatly pruned bushes. By virtue of their form and flower—perfected over centuries of breeding—roses can hold their own when planted solo. But if that's the only way you know roses, you don't know what you're missing.

Roses are adaptable. They can crown nearly any type of garden from the formal to the most casual. Perfect border companions, many are well behaved and sophisticated enough for city courtyards. Others will gracefully adorn a suburban porch or a country yard.

Even if your garden is of a more practical nature, don't dismiss the idea of a planting of roses. Herb and vegetable gardens have long been welcome spots for the rose, which is, after all, an herb. No matter what type of garden you have, there's a rose that fits in and lifts it above the ordinary.

OPPOSITE: Aside from color and fragrance, roses contribute their own inimitable form to the border garden. The grandiflora 'Queen Elizabeth' explodes in billows of pink blooms, while white-flowered 'Marie Pavie' presents a more upright, twiggy look. *Rosa multifora* var. *carnea* shows the classic rosebush shape.

RIGHT: Roses form a wall of riotous color that seems to heighten the severe effect of box parterres in this herb garden, making the shades of green seem even more vivid. While we think of the rose as purely ornamental, it is in fact a true herb that has been used medicinally for many centuries.

ABOVE: Imagine a Texas evening with the sun setting and the fragrant scent of roses wafting over the porch. Porch surrounds are the perfect places to plant roses. They'll hide an unsightly concrete foundation, at the same time providing an inspiring view.

ABOVE: Don't be fooled into thinking that roses belong only within the confines of a refined bed or classic cottage garden. Even in the dry and wild West, Austrian briar (*Rosa foetida*) seems at home in a front yard garden.

206

ABOVE: Where architectural lines are straight and materials are simple—such as the adobe and timber of this pueblo-style house—a single rosebush in the court-yard adds color and softens the stark effect. Even in areas with little rainfall, drought- and heat-tolerant roses can be found to ornament the garden.

ABOVE: Roses are quite at home in a formal setting, surrounded by a well-tended lawn and clipped box hedges. The mix of colors found here keeps the planting lively.

RIGHT: A small walled garden seems to be a perfect spot for roses. Ramblers cling to the wall, softening the effect without detracting from the tall spires of foxglove.

LEFT: With their glowing blossoms held high, roses always attract attention. They're dramatic enough to be admired from afar, and can be planted some distance from the house without diminishing their effect.

BELOW: Here, structure is provided by a fountain and sharply edged beds. Luminous white roses spill over the slate edging, adding soft curves to make the garden more welcoming.

ABOVE: A plain garden path can be transformed with the addition of a simple pergola and a few climbing roses. An understory of herbaceous perennials serves to accent the roses 'Botany Bay' and 'Ballerina'.

OPPOSITE: Shrub roses can serve as specimen plants in the landscape. Here, a 'Charles Austin' rosebush boldly stands alone, letting the grace of its flowers claim the attention.

ABOVE: Roses are citizens of the world, at home in any domain. Rambling roses growing against a brick wall exude a rambunctious flair that fits in perfectly with a wild meadow.

LEFT: Roses have a long and storied history in British landscapes. Here, a vibrant pink 'Cockade' rose grows up an arched arbor, offering a focal point in a kitchen garden.

LEFT: With careful selection, roses can serve as landscape highlights for three seasons of the year. A long-blooming rose, such as this musk, will continue to flower well into autumn, until frost etches its blooms.

BELOW: There may be nothing more enchanting than an exuberant white garden, with blooms tumbling like sea foam, in a formal setting. The roses 'Sombreuil' and 'Pearl Drift' carry off this effect beautifully.

RIGHT: A single rose can have powerful impact when it is trained as a standard. This shining example drifts like a cloud over an underplanting of herbs, including hyssop, thyme, sorrel, and fragrant lavender.

BELOW: Sometimes it's best to just throw caution (and budget) to the wind, and let roses dazzle in their full grandeur. A bold sweep of several varieties along a path is held in place by a yellow-green band of alchemilla.

ABOVE: The country garden requires a thoughtful approach that appears unplanned. Rambling and climbing roses, with their wild flavor, make ideal foundations for such naturalistic plantings.

LEFT: Balance and repetition are important in formal gardens, but that doesn't have to mean a redundancy of plants. Here, a prolific white rose shrub is mirrored by a shapely *Acer* 'Bloodgood' across the path, lending an imaginative harmony to the scene.

ABOVE: In some landscapes, roses are meant to be the main feature. A small, well-mulched bed, carved from a lawn, shows a variety of shrub roses to their best advantage.

OPPOSITE: Clinging to a trellis that mirrors the garden pool, a pair of climbing roses adds a new dimension of color and form to a simple courtyard. Subtle rock garden plants warm the space without detracting from the glory of the roses.

Part Four

ORNAMENTAL GRASSES

INTRODUCTION

Unique among garden plants, ornamental grasses have a special relation-ship with nature. Whether dancing and glistening in the late afternoon sun, swaying sensuously with the gentlest summer breeze, or melodiously rustling by the edge of a pond, grasses respond with unparalleled intimacy to the subtle changes of the seasons, delightfully intensifying an appreciation of the natural life cycle of the garden.

Offering both beauty and hardiness, today's palette of ornamental grasses includes myriad variations in size, form, texture, and color with grasses available to suit almost any purpose in the garden. Diminutive gems can serve as delicate garden accents, while midsize species can fill niches commonly reserved for speci-men shrubs or hedges, and the tallest species, growing as much as fifteen feet (4.5m) in a single season, can have the presence of small trees. Shapes and forms also run the full gamut, with strictly upright grasses perfect for creating dramatic exclamation points, gently arching types useful for connecting adjacent plantings, and low spreaders offering superb ground cover possibilities. In addition, grass textures cover a wide range, from as coarse as corn to as fine as feathers. The spectrum of grass colors is also broad, with snow white, pearlescent pink, and purple-bronze blooms lasting from midsummer through autumn. When sun-dried, the flowers become silvery plumes that frequently remain attractive throughout winter. Foliage colors of countless tones of green, white, yellow, blue, and red make an appearance in summer, followed by an autumn array of golds, burnt-umbers, and burgundies.

Ornamental grasses are among the easiest to grow of all perennial plants. Although the majority prefer sunny sites, they are otherwise adaptable to a wide range of soil, temperature, and moisture conditions and are relatively disease- and pest-free. Their fibrous root systems are very efficient, making most grasses extremely drought tolerant. For the most part, maintenance consists of a once-yearly cutting back, plus occasionally dividing the plants to renew vigor.

Whether your garden is modest or vast, formal or informal, or in a dry or rainy climate, the beauty, diversity, and ease of gardening with ornamental grasses offer splendid opportunities to increase your gardening pleasure.

ABOVE: The silvery plumes of ravenna grass, *Erianthus ravennae*, shoot skyward in mid-autumn, silhouetted by the sun.

OPPOSITE: Stripped of their seeds by winter's end, plumes of *Miscanthus* 'Graziella' are fixed in a gentle wave.

THE UNIQUE BEAUTY OF ORNAMENTAL GRASSES

*B*y gardening with ornamental grasses, a gardener's focus must naturally shift slightly away from color, and emphasis must be placed on such features as translucency, line, form, texture, scale, variegation, and seasonal interest. By developing a sensitivity to the unique attributes of grasses and using their features to their full advantage in the blueprint or planning stages of your garden, you will reap the most rewards when gardening with these unusual plants. As a rule of thumb, grasses are particularly effective when backlit by the sun; their translucent foliage and flowers shimmer and glow. Although a few grasses are wide-leaved and bold, most have strong-lined, narrow foliage that provides stunning contrast to broad-leaved companion plants. In addition, grasses are at their best when intermingled with other types of perennials and with shrubs and trees. Most remain effective long after the growing season ends; their splendid autumn tones weather gracefully to winter hues of chestnut, fawn, and russet, making them ideal neighbors to brightly berried shrubs and trees with ornamental bark. Allow the grasses to extend your garden's appeal throughout the year.

OPPOSITE: Side-lit by the autumn sun, the narrow plumes of feather-reed grass, *Calamagrostis* 'Karl Foerster', glow like candles. This grass retains its delicate translucency through winter, when the streaming rays of the sun strike a low angle. Coaxed by the wind, individual plumes move in and out of the sun streams, creating a magical flickering effect.

ABOVE: The flowers of mellic grass, *Melica ciliata*, are brilliantly illuminated when backlit by the early summer sun. The shadows behind the plant provide a dark contrast and enhance the radiance of the flowers, adding depth and texture to the scene.

TOP: Strong lines drawn by the foliage of grasses are most effective when contrasted against dark spaces or bold objects. Here, creating a stunningly crosshatched natural window frame, the daggerlike leaves of porcupine grass, *Miscanthus* 'Strictus', reveal just enough of the view beyond to excite the imagination.

ABOVE: The variegated foliage of this *Miscanthus* 'Morning Light' creates a flowing fountainlike effect that epitomizes the graceful beauty of ornamental grasses. The finely linear foliage of the grass is strikingly juxtaposed with its broad-leafed and bold-textured companions.

LEFT: The coarse texture and large scale of giant reed, *Arundo donax*, make this grass an appropriate match for this distinctive English dwelling. The grass boldly competes with the large flowers of the hydrangea, and the plant's upright, vertical growth creates a nice counterpoint to the vine trailing horizontally in the background.

ABOVE: Oblique lighting accentuates the dramatic form of this tall moor grass, *Molinia* 'Karl Foerster'. Dense and irregular in shape, the backdrop of richly textured conifers showcases the ordered filaments of the grass, seemingly holding the grass flowers aloft. Although this arrangement is painted entirely in greens, it has great depth and contrast.

ABOVE: Color can be the most compelling aspect of some grasses. Here, the teal foliage of this fescue, *Festuca* 'Meerblau', combines with the carmine and pink-flowered heathers to create a beautiful palette of ground covers. The tufted mounds of the grass are also complemented by the carefree form of the heather.

LEFT: This ribbon of Japanese bloodgrass, *Imperata* 'Red Baron', mixed with variegated meadow foxtail, *Alopecurus pratensis* 'Variegatus', creates an exuberant, arresting border.

ABOVE: Variegated grasses offer exciting opportunities for brightening secluded, shady corners or providing distinct focal points in garden compositions. Here, the classic symmetry of variegated giant reed, *Arundo donax* 'Variegata', creates a piece of living sculpture.

OPPOSITE: Stirring gently in a summer breeze, dancing before an autumn storm, or flying in a spring gale, grasses mirror nature's moods, bringing a special dynamism to the garden. Here, New Zealand grasses paint a portrait in the wind.

OPPOSITE: The platinum and silver plumes of ornamental grasses make ideal companions for the brilliant autumn foliage of deciduous trees and shrubs. Here, pampas grass, *Cortaderia selloana*, enhances the rich scarlet of a mountain ash.

ABOVE: Many grasses are wondrously colored in autumn. Although green in summer, the leaves of this wild oat, *Chasmanthium latifolium*, become golden licks of flame in autumn, and the intricate detail of the oatlike seed-heads is marvelously revealed by the late-season backlighting.

ABOVE AND RIGHT: Frost follows the graceful lines of these mixed grasses in two views of a steel-gray English morning. Nodding heads of thistles echo the grasses' cascading foliage, and dark tree trunks create an aura of intrigue and mystery. Few garden plants meet the end of the growing season with such serene beauty.

ABOVE: The rigors of winter fail to diminish the magnificence of ornamental grasses. Encrusted with ice in a late-winter storm, this *Miscanthus* drips with jewel-like crystals.

LEFT: This *Miscanthus* seed-head emerged in late summer as a flag of coppery flowers, matured through autumn into a downy plume, and closed winter as this stunning filigree. Although the seed-head is delicate, its life could be further extended if used in an arrangement of dried flowers.

FORMAL LANDSCAPES

*D*iverse in form and function, ornamental grasses are equally at home in formal and informal garden designs. Although there is no definitive distinction between the two styles, formal landscapes are usually characterized by orderly plantings often built around distinct axes or symmetries. In formal designs, grasses may be used as focal points, as specimens for accent, or in ordered sweeps or patterns.

RIGHT: Grasses are often at their best near water. With its rounded form artfully fitted to the curve of the stone coping, this magnificent specimen of *Miscanthus* 'Morning Light' makes a stunning focal point for a corner of an elegant pool. The finely variegated cascading foliage is subtly mirrored in the still water, surrounded by the billowy reflections of the nearby trees.

OPPOSITE: In this interior courtyard, lush sweeps of *Molinia* and *Sesleria* flow effortlessly behind the curvilinear design of a retaining wall, creating a living sea of green. In the foreground, the tawny heads of *Koeleria* resemble a miniature prairie. Even though the space is modest and the planting is highly ordered, the fine texture and inherent detail of the grasses give the visual impression of a vast landscape with a sense of natural abandon.

ABOVE: The blue-gray foliage of blue oat grass, *Helictotrichon sempervirens*, makes a handsome combination with the low formal hedge of 'Crimson Pygmy' barberry. This duo has great staying power, since both plants retain their foliage color from spring through late autumn. The oat grass will add its delicate flower spikes to the scene in early summer; however, in this mid-spring view, the floral interest is provided by pink-purple tulips interplanted with the grass. Many bulbs, such as crocuses and daffodils, coexist happily with ornamental grasses. After the bulbs flower in the spring, their foliage is neatly masked by the subsequent growth of the grasses.

LEFT: In this art-form California garden, the single fountain grass, *Pennisetum alopecuroides*, serves a sculptural purpose, its rounded form mimicking the bluish yuccas. The sweeps of succulents and sharp turns of the walls and planting beds impart an austere, angular feeling to the design, with the grass adding a welcome softness.

ABOVE: A classic greensward and close-clipped evergreens define these highly formal flower borders, yet the patch of tufted hair grass, *Deschampsia cespitosa*, seems quite appropriate to the design. Airy and cloudlike, the straw-colored flowers of the grass add levity to the ordered landscape and accentuate the sculpted beauty of the evergreens and the antique urn.

LEFT: An intimate path leads to this hidden pool surrounded by Japanese umbrella pines. This secret garden is graced by a river of purple barberry flowing down a slope, leading the eye to focus on a large specimen of fountain grass, *Pennisetum alopecuroides*, nestling against a tall *Iris pseudacorus*. Although neither is in flower, the contrasting forms and textures of these two plants make for a beautifully balanced composition.

OPPOSITE: The tall lines of this variegated giant reed, *Arundo donax* 'Variegata', provide a boldly formal focal point in an otherwise loosely planted courtyard garden.

ABOVE: This exuberant studio garden makes delightful use of annuals, perennials, and tender species to create a richly colored composition. Short and tufted blue fescue, *Festuca ovina* var. *glauca*, and tall and feathery blue oat grass, *Helictotrichon sempervirens*, contribute exquisite steel-blues to the palette.

LEFT: A magnificent specimen of golden variegated pampas grass, *Cortaderia* 'Gold Band', anchors this traditional English-style flower border. The brightly striped foliage of the grass is in perfect harmony with the border's yellow color scheme, and the cascading foliage contrasts effectively with the vertical flower spikes of the silver mulleins.

ABOVE LEFT: The massive trunks of Chilean wine palms contribute to the otherworldly feeling of this Southern California garden. The pervading color scheme is carried successfully from alternating ground cover sweeps of blue senecio and the lower mounds of blue fescue grass, *Festuca ovina* var. *glauca*, to the fan-shaped leaves of blue hesper palms above.

ABOVE RIGHT: This contemporary garden in Japan consists almost entirely of sculpted evergreen trees and shrubs. Although much of the garden is shaded in late afternoon, sunbeams brightly illuminate the copper flowers of a specimen *Miscanthus*, which serves as the central unifying element in the garden's design. Native to Japan, *Miscanthus* is a traditional Japanese emblem of autumn.

OPPOSITE TOP: The bold-textured flowers of purple clematis in this English border are perfect foils for the feathery plumes of *Pennisetum villosum*, the brightest white of all the fountain grasses. The ample width of the stone paving allows the grass to spill voluptuously into the walkway.

OPPOSITE BOTTOM: This sunken garden combines a formally symmetrical paving design with relatively unstructured plantings, evoking the romanticism of a garden ruin. Although there are a number of ornamental grasses in the picture, they are discreetly and effectively incorporated into the composition. Some serve as focal points, others provide fine-textured contrast, and still others are employed solely for the color of their foliage.

INFORMAL LANDSCAPES

*I*nherently informal, the flowing foliage of ornamental grasses and the carefree abandon of their flowers often seem ideal choices when the design intent is to create a casual mood, subtly suggestive of natural, unstudied landscapes.

RIGHT: On a hazy midsummer's day, this understated border plays gently with the sunlight and gracefully meets the pastoral landscape beyond. The bold forms of purple coneflower and globe thistle are distinct against the soft mass of switch grass, *Panicum virgatum*. Behind the grass, sedums and the orbicular foliage of giant coneflower provide additional textural variety.

OPPOSITE: Grasses and sedges consort in seemingly random fashion around this small naturalistic pond. The dark sheet of water balances the airiness of the grasses while the water lilies contrast with the grass foliage in both form and texture. The rough-hewn stones edging the pond contribute to the casual mood, adding to the illusion that this garden is an uncontrived part of the native landscape.

ABOVE: This late-autumn glimpse of the border shown on the previous page details its magical transformation into a vibrantly colored tribute to the season. At left, the switch grass, *Panicum virgatum*, has turned golden yellow, as have the leaves of the giant coneflower. *Miscanthus* 'Purpurascens' is now the star of the border, and its dark orange foliage and silvery plumes are stunning in combination with the blackish seed-heads of the coneflower and the rich wine color of the sedum.

RIGHT: Ingeniously placed grasses lend a naturalness and intimacy to this backyard patio that belie the garden's semi-urban location. The fine texture of porcupine grass, *Miscanthus* 'Strictus', is particularly effective in association with the large leaves of the plume poppy and the dark tree trunks.

ABOVE: Ornamental grasses can be employed to create a natural screen, blocking unwanted views or restructuring garden spaces in much the same way a hedge or shrub border might be used. Here, a semi-circular sweep of feather-reed grass, *Calamagrostis* 'Karl Foerster', defines a private space under the spreading branches of a honey locust, providing a delightful spot for outdoor dining.

ABOVE AND RIGHT: Identical views of the same garden taken one month apart dramatically illustrate the alchemy of perennial borders that include a mixture of ornamental grasses. In early summer (*above*), floral fountains of mellic grass, *Melica ciliata*, adorn the rustic stone path while pink roses reach their blooming peak. Later (*right*), the mellic grass assumes a minor role in a tapestry of greens as a river of blue lyme grass, *Elymus arenarius*, rises to become a focal point accompanied by bright yellow daylilies.

ABOVE: The subtle foliage and flower colors of dormant grasses provide a matchless background for displaying the subdued winter hues of companion plants. A tawny background sweep of *Miscanthus* beautifully sets off the striped foliage and intricate seed pods of variegated yuccas.

OPPOSITE: Tucked behind seed-heads of orange coneflower in a tiny urban garden, this feather-reed grass, *Calamagrostis* 'Karl Foerster', is dazzlingly illuminated by just a few sun rays threading through the leaves of a neighboring maple.

ABOVE: As companion flowers ebb and flow, this border is continually brightened by a spreading mass of ribbon grass, *Phalaris arundinacea* 'Picta'.

OPPOSITE: A huge specimen of silver feather grass, *Miscanthus* 'Silberfeder', is magnificently framed by dark green conifers. The cascading form of the grass gives it particular charm.

ABOVE: Pampas grasses glow in the diffuse, romantic light of an English autumn. Among the most imposing of ornamental grasses, these plants can take the place of small trees in the landscape.

LEFT: Many drought-tolerant ornamental grasses are adapted to even the driest climates. Growing alongside native penstemons, this *Muhlenbergia* grass is a wonderful foil for the bold saguaro cacti silhouetted in the background of this Arizona desert garden.

OPPOSITE: Moisture-loving primroses, sedges, and irises make a pleasing foreground mosaic as variegated manna grass, *Glyceria maxima* 'Variegata', ventures out into the water, providing a light contrast with the magenta azalea.

GRASSES IN NATIVE LANDSCAPES

*G*rasses are an integral part of the drama of contrasting textures, forms, colors, and illumination that is common to many native landscapes. Whether your design preference is formal or informal, an awareness of natural patterns will provide inspiration for integrating grasses into your own landscape.

TOP LEFT: Reminiscent of the once vast midwestern prairies, this autumnal blanket woven from broomsedge, *Andropogon virginicus*, and little bluestem, *Schizachyrium scoparium*, grows naturally in this field on the east coast of the United States.

BOTTOM LEFT: Infused with a golden glow in a sunny autumn meadow, this switch grass, *Panicum virgatum*, is highlighted against the muted forest beyond.

OPPOSITE: These grand sweeps of switch grass, *Panicum virgatum*, followed by the taller common reed, *Phragmites australis*, are the natural result of varying moisture on this sloping ground in New York State. In wild landscapes, grasses frequently occur in masses, and these natural formations are effective models for larger garden designs. The silvery monochrome of the grasses is in sublime balance with the brilliant autumn foliage colors of this East Coast deciduous forest.

ABOVE: Billowy clouds of crinkled hair grass, *Deschampsia flexuosa,* tumble over massive black granite boulders high in the Blue Ridge Mountains. This dynamic combination eloquently suggests similar juxtapositions in the gardened landscape.

LEFT: Even in cold climates, the beauty of wild grasses transcends the dimming effect of winter. Both lithe and resilient, little bluestem, *Schizachyrium scoparium,* recovers here from midwinter snows to paint a hillside with its fawns and russets.

ABOVE: Native to the coastal mountains of southern California, deergrass, *Muhlenbergia rigens*, beautiful-ly adorns distinctive boulders dramatically arrayed among live oaks. The low angle of the late-winter sun impressively sidelights both grass and stone.

ABOVE: Here, huge burnished tufts of *Chionochloa rubra* are splayed by powerful winds sweeping the interior mountains of New Zealand's south island.

CONTRASTING ELEMENTS

F̶ew gardens consist solely of plants; the most satisfying compositions make imaginative decorative use of other elements. These may be natural or man-made, luxuries or necessities, fixed features or movable objects. Ornamental grasses work well when combined with other elements in the garden, however their airy, fine-textured qualities are especially effective when associated with features of greater density and weight.

STAIRS, STEPS, AND WALKWAYS

RIGHT: This west-facing stone walk leads directly into the setting autumn sun, which splendidly backlights the foliage and flowers of wild oat, *Chasmanthium latifolium.*

OPPOSITE: Whenever possible, build garden walkways wide enough to allow grasses and other border plants to spill over them. Laden with raindrops, the rich mix of grasses and perennials in this intimate English garden have discreetly pushed their way over the cut stone walk.

ABOVE: Soft to the touch as well as to the eye, the arching flowers of these mellic grasses, *Melica ciliata*, complement the curves of this weathered fieldstone walkway.

LEFT: Beginning in the foreground, fountain grass, *Pennisetum alopecuroides, Spodiopogon sibiricus,* and tall moor grass, *Molinia* 'Transparent', alternate with bolder sedums and coneflowers to create a handsomely varied framework for this simple bluestone walk.

ABOVE: This concrete stairway might seem too heavy for this garden if not for the softening effect of the ornamental grasses. Beginning along the pathway, a plumed procession of fountain grass, *Pennisetum orientale;* Korean feather-reed grass, *Calamagrostis arundinacea* var. *brachytricha;* and *Miscanthus* 'Purpurascens' gracefully ascends the stairs. Small containers of scarlet geraniums provide pointed accents of color.

ABOVE RIGHT: The loosely pendulous, illuminated spikelets of wild oat, *Chasmanthium latifolium,* are the perfect complement to the precise stone steps leading over the water in this intimate pool garden.

FENCES, GATES, AND WALLS

ABOVE: Here, the elegant flower stalks of tall moor grass, *Molinia* 'Windspiel', admirably ease the transition from a sturdy white-painted fence to a rustic bridge crossing a small stream just beyond.

LEFT: This doorway dramatically frames a specimen *Miscanthus* 'Purpurascens'. The luminous grass beckons visitors to pass through the portal into the sun-drenched landscape beyond.

ABOVE: A simple split-rail fence takes on a sculptural quality when backed by a solid chestnut-colored sweep of native grasses. The fence might be functional, marking a property line between neighbor's fields, or it might be an artful contrivance used to signal the division between a formal mowed section of garden and a less manicured area deliberately sown with native grasses. In either case, the fallen rail adds a charming bit of disorder.

LEFT: When planted en masse, fountain grasses, *Pennisetum alopecuroides*, and orange coneflowers superbly balance the weight of this solid stone wall.

OPPOSITE: A tidy and neatly contained row of ribbon grass, *Phalaris arundinacea* 'Picta', brightens the base of this dry-laid fieldstone wall. The white variegation in the foliage of the grass echoes the white flower puffs of *Fothergilla*.

GARDEN FURNITURE, SCULPTURE, AND ARCHITECTURE

ABOVE: Mature specimens of various *Miscanthus* grasses provide privacy on this otherwise open, sunny stone patio. With the sun's rays lapping at these chaise longues, this secluded hideaway will be cherished as summer breezes whisper through the grasses.

RIGHT: Man-made objects with strong forms, such as this antique iron wheel, create a wonderful dynamic with grasses. Placed here with Indian grass, *Sorghastrum nutans*, and goldenrods in a naturalistic meadow garden, the rusty wheel creates a setting evocative of a pastoral landscape that is all-too-quickly vanishing.

ABOVE: A large *Miscanthus* 'Gracillimus' in full bloom gracefully connects this deck to the ground and water below. The cascading grass acts to accentuate the strong horizontal lines of the porch.

ABOVE: The explosive form of this Korean feather-reed grass, *Calamagrostis arundinacea* var. *brachytricha*, stands in bold contrast with the refined, rounded form of a small gazebo.

ABOVE: This poolside setting showcases feather-reed grass, *Calamagrostis* 'Karl Foerster'. The height of the grass is accentuated by the broad surface of the water and lower-growing coneflowers and fountain grasses, while the masses of crimson barberry and a purple beech behind provide dark contrast with the tawny flowers of the grass.

ABOVE: An allee of pleached linden trees introduces an intriguing horizontal line to this landscape, contrasting with both the steeply pitched roof of the building and the relaxed flowing form of the Korean feather-reed grass, *Calamagrostis arundinacea* var. *brachytricha*. This garden ingeniously intermingles vegetables and traditional ornamental plants: red-stemmed Swiss chard is visible through the feathery plumes of the grass.

STONES

ABOVE: Fountains of blue oat grass, *Helictotrichon sempervirens,* flow freely from stone crevices in this New York State rock garden. Although the scene is entirely contrived, it borrows directly from innumerable natural models where delicate grasses are intermingled with coarse boulders.

DECORATIVE CONTAINERS

ABOVE: The enduring foliage color of ornamental grasses ideally suits them for use in decorative containers. This coal-black urn showcases a brightly variegated *Miscanthus*, providing an imposing focal point at the end of a rich tapestry of flowering herbaceous plants and colorful shrubs.

LEFT: Set against a backdrop of Japanese red maple, this container combination of blue oat grass, *Helictotrichon sempervirens*, and purple setcreasea is satisfying all summer long.

275

ABOVE: Almost any grass can be displayed in a container if given sufficient space for root development. Here, mature specimens of *Miscanthus* 'Purpurascens' are edged with small blue fescues in these large wooden containers and are still quite beautiful even in late autumn.

LEFT: The wine-red color of this purple fountain grass, *Pennisetum setaceum* 'Rubrum', would be welcome in many areas of the garden and can be easily relocated due to the versatility of this modest-size container.

BOLD-TEXTURED COMPANION PLANTS

ABOVE: This elegant and dramatic combination balances the relatively fine-textured foliage of *Miscanthus* with the gargantuan leaves of *Petasites*.

ABOVE: The most compelling gardens are often created by the apparent collision of disparate styles. Here, immaculately clipped conical yews, the quintessence of formal horticulture, are unusually arresting awash in the informality of *Miscanthus*.

RIGHT: The bold, dried flowers of this ornamental thistle make a stirring combination with the tightly tufted foliage of blue fescue.

ABOVE: In an appealing combination, the delicate autumn plumes of Korean feather-reed grass, *Calamagrostis arundinacea* var. *brachytricha*, lean affectionately on the strong shoulders of a burgundy-colored sedum.

OPPOSITE: Fountains of fine *Pennisetum* foliage are striking when placed opposite the dinner plate–size flower heads and rugged leaves of a cow-parsnip.

ABOVE: This needle grass, *Stipa pulchra*, is too subtle to be effective by itself, but in combination with these bright orange California poppies, the grass makes a bold statement in this simple but eye-catching scene.

OPPOSITE: Here, a giant plume poppy towers over a tropically luxuriant specimen of porcupine grass, *Miscanthus* 'Strictus'. The orange coneflowers add a touch of bright color.

ABOVE: Colorful foliage of variegated Hakone grass, *Hakonechloa macra* 'Aureola', blends harmoniously with the bright daisylike flowers of a *Senecio*, while various foliage textures are richly contrasted in this artfully composed border.

OPPOSITE: Experiment with all manners of bold-textured plants when choosing companions for your grasses. These prickly pear cacti are surprisingly successful mates to this variegated *Miscanthus*.

285

PHOTO CREDITS

©Philip Beaurline: pp. 85, 86 left

©Crandall & Crandall: 186 right, 217

©Rick Darke: pp. 220, 221, 222, 223, 224–225 all, 226, 227 both, 228, 231, 233 both, 234, 235, 236–237 all, 238 both, 239, 241 right, 242 both, 243 both, 244, 245, 246–247 all, 248, 249 both, 250, 251, 256, 257 both, 258–259 all, 260, 261, 262, 263, 264–265 all, 266 both, 267 both, 268, 269 bottom, 270–271, 272 both, 273 both, 274, 275 both, 276 right, 277, 278–279 all, 280, 281, 282, 283, 284

©Alan Detrick: p. 176 left

©Alan & Linda Detrick: p. 190 right

©Ken Druse: pp. 92 left, 122, 125, 145, 147 left

©Derek Fell: pp. 27, 29, 41, 169, 172, 178, 270 left, 276 left

©John Glover: pp. 20, 23, 25, 28, 30 left, 30–31, 42, 48, 49, 50 left, 58 both, 61 top and bottom left, 65 left, 74, 75 both, 76, 77, 79 both, 101, 102, 103 both, 104 left, 107 both, 113 top, 123 left, 132 left, 135, 139, 140 both, 142, 144 right, 147 right, 148–149, 154 left, 173 left, 202 right, 230, 232 both, 253, 254 top, 255, 285

©Bruce Jenkins/Full Frame: p. 229

©Dency Kane: pp. 2, 8, 9, 10, 11, 12, 32, 33, 52, 57, 61 top right, 63 both, 64 both, 119, 129, 132–133,

134 right, 144 left, 180, 185, 187 left, 188 right, 190 left, 197 right, 203 bottom, 204, 218–19

©image/dennis krukowski: p. 89

©Charles Mann: pp. 22, 34, 44, 59, 60, 62, 86 right, 87, 88, 91, 98, 99, 100 right, 104–105, 106, 110–111, 112, 114–115, 120 bottom, 143, 155 right, 163 left, 206 both, 207, 208 top, 214 bottom, 215 top, 216, 240–241, 254 bottom

©Clive Nichols: pp. 5, 6, 16, 17, 18, 19, 21, 24, 26, 27, 35, 36, 38, 39, 40, 45, 46–47, 47 right, 50–51, 53, 54–55, 56, 65 right, 66, 67, 68 all, 69, 70, 71, 72 both, 73, 84, 90, 92 right, 93, 94, 95, 96, 97, 116, 121, 127, 128, 134 left, 136, 137 both, 138, 148, 150–151, 152, 153, 155 left, 156, 157, 158 both, 159, 160 both, 161, 162, 163 right, 164, 166, 168, 170 both, 171 both, 173 right, 174, 175 both, 176 right, 177, 179, 181, 182 both, 183, 184 both, 186 left, 188 left, 189 both, 191 both, 192, 193, 194 both, 195, 196 both, 198 both, 199, 200 both, 201 both, 202 left, 208 bottom, 209 both, 210, 211, 212 both, 213 both, 214 top, 215 bottom

©Jerry Pavia: pp. 43, 55 right, 100 left, 108 left, 111, 113 bottom, 114 left, 120 top, 123 right, 124, 126, 131 right, 141, 143 right, 146, 154 right, 165, 167, 187 right, 197 right, 203 top, 205

©Richard Shiell: pp. 108–109, 117, 118, 130–131

©Nance Trueworthy: pp. 14, 78, 80, 81

©Cynthia Woodyard: p. 269 top

INDEX